T0245598

AIRCRAFT, TANKS & ARTILLERY
OF THE UKRAINE WAR

AIRCRAFT, TANKS & ARTILLERY
OF THE UKRAINE WAR

MARTIN J. DOUGHERTY

amber
BOOKS

Published by Amber Books Ltd
United House
London N7 9DP
United Kingdom
www.amberbooks.co.uk
Facebook: amberbooks
YouTube: amberbooksltd
Instagram: amberbooksltd
X(Twitter): @amberbooks

ISBN: 978-1-83886-350-0

Editor: Michael Spilling
Designer: Keren Harragan & Andrew Easton
Picture research: Terry Forshaw

Printed in China

Contents

Introduction

The breakup of the Soviet Union in 1991 resulted in 15 new countries, of which Russia was by far the largest and most powerful. Military hardware was divided among the successor states, creating a situation in which multiple countries possessed identical equipment and training. Not all of this equipment was in a good state of repair, however. Lack of investment in the last years of the Soviet Union forced obsolescent designs to soldier on, and matters did not improve after the dissolution of the Soviet Union.

The reputation of Russia as a military superpower suffered in these years, with prestigious warships retired or sold off incomplete and few new systems appearing to replace the obsolescent Soviet-era hardware. Improving economic conditions eventually allowed Russia to begin implementing a new generation of weaponry. Notably, the advanced features of the T-14 Armata main battle tank were proudly shown off to the world, with the subtext that Russia had regained its status at the forefront of military power.

In the meantime, Russia still waged wars, though of relatively low intensity. Fighting in Chechnya and Georgia, while at times bloody, did not require the resources of a superpower, nor did intervention in Syria. In these cases, Russia was able to select which formations were most suitable rather than committing a large force that would more accurately reflect the state of its military as a whole.

The annexation of Crimea in 2014 did not meet significant resistance. Ukraine was at the time suffering internal political troubles and could not have responded effectively as Russian forces occupied key points. The annexation resulted in sanctions against Russia but no overseas intervention. This is often seen as the beginning of the Ukraine/Russian conflict, though at the time many considered the situation would settle into a tense but tolerable status quo. Ukrainian forces did attempt to counter the separatist movement in the east of the country, engaging Russian-backed separatist groups that

Russia's incursions into Ukrainian territory began in 2014, with the annexation of the Crimean peninsula and the support of separatist forces in the Donbas region in the east of the country.

Ukraine conflict areas of control, September 2014

- Annexed by Russia, February–March 2014
- Controlled by pro-Russian/Russian forces, September 2014
- Under Ukrainian government control

U K R A I N E

R U S S I A

Sea of Azov

CRIMEA

0   100 km

0   100 miles

N

had seized several cities. In addition to supplying arms to these groups, Russia offered political support and sent large numbers of 'volunteers' to join the fighting. Despite reports of skirmishes and incursions by Russian troops, the situation was stabilized with an agreement between Ukraine and Russia.

This turned out to be the first of many ceasefires and agreements regarding the region, none of which survived. The situation in the east became static, with fighting between trench lines interspersed with raids and shelling. Russian forces were reported to be present in eastern Ukraine, while the recruiting of fighters to join the separatists was commonplace. The most effective units of the Ukrainian armed forces were still engaged in this conflict at the time of the Russian invasion.

It may be that Russia always intended to invade Ukraine, though the conflict could be an example of 'mission creep' on a vast scale. Either way, some Russian actions on the wider world stage can be interpreted as intended to create suitable conditions for an invasion of Ukraine, and there is evidence of cyberwarfare along with psychological operations in the political arena. However, even as Russian troops massed close to the Ukrainian border, there was hope this latest crisis would be defused.

Russia invades

In February 2022, the conflict in the Donbas region escalated significantly. On 23 February, Russia announced it would recognize the separatist-held regions and sent troops into Donbas on what was described as a peacekeeping mission. The following

A Ukrainian T-64 main battle tank in the Donetsk region, 2022. Blocks of explosive reactive armour (ERA) enhance its armour protection against shaped-charge anti-tank weapons.

day, the invasion began. There was no formal declaration of war; the conflict was presented as a 'special military operation'. At first glance, the outcome may have seemed a foregone conclusion. In the north, armoured columns advanced towards Kharkov and the capital, Kyiv. Forces deployed from Crimea were tasked with capturing critical port cities. The most effective elements of the Ukrainian army were deployed in the east, where they came under attack from Russian formations deployed to the Donbas region. The ground offensive was accompanied by air and missile strikes against military targets and infrastructure.

Despite predictions that Kyiv would fall quickly, Russian forces ran into stiff resistance all along their advance, culminating in combat in the outskirts of the capital. In particular, infantry anti-tank weapons played a critical role in grinding down Russia's armoured vehicle strength and slowing the advance. Logistical problems also played a part.

It may be that Russian planners were overconfident and failed to prepare for the massive logistical effort required to support such large forces in a sustained battle. There have also been suggestions that the internal affairs of the Russian army were to blame, with formations over-declaring their readiness to avoid punishment and then struggling to complete their missions somehow.

Ukrainian counteroffensives and international support

Whatever the reasons, the Russian advance was slowed then pushed back in the north, and by April, there was no longer an immediate threat to the capital. Later in the year, a Ukrainian counteroffensive drove Russian forces back in the north, after which the fighting was confined to the south and east. In the meantime, Russian forces captured several key cities in the south before being pushed back across the Dnipro River. After a pause over the winter, a further Ukrainian counteroffensive regained more ground, albeit slowly.

A key factor in the success of Ukrainian forces was the arrival of weaponry and ammunition from overseas. This was a complex and difficult process resulting in protests from Moscow. Arguably, the arrival of large numbers of anti-tank weapons was the most significant event of the conflict. These not only enabled Ukrainian forces to halt the Russian advance but demonstrated that Ukraine could survive. The old adage 'do not reinforce defeat' was an obstacle to supporting Ukraine – nations might not wish to anger Russia over a lost cause.

These weapons helped Ukraine avoid defeat and bought time,

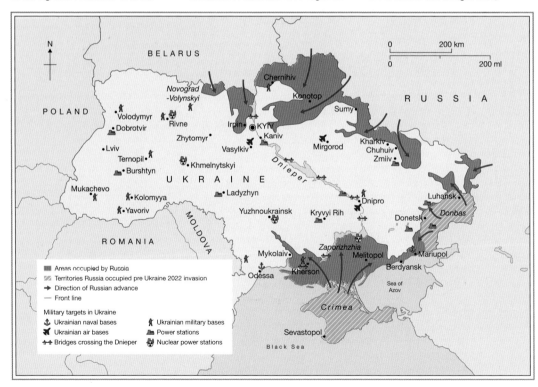

Advancing from positions in the occupied Donbas region, Crimea and neighbouring Belarus, the Russian offensive reached the outskirts of the Ukrainian capital Kyiv before being driven back. The map shows the extent of the Russian advances on 7 March 2022.

allowing others to arrive. These included tanks and fighter jets, but perhaps the most significant was long-range artillery. These weapons allowed Ukraine to strike at bases and logistical assets previously out of reach. The materiel damage was significant, but there were wider implications. Russian commanders were forced to choose between leaving their ammunition dumps vulnerable or expending time and effort protecting them. This absorbed manpower and resources at a time when both were in short supply and increased the logistics burden.

Character of the conflict

It might have been expected that Russian forces would engage in sweeping armoured assaults intended to encircle and cut off key targets. Such operations have been part of Russian doctrine since World War II, and much of the Russian army's equipment still reflects this. However, the ground offensives had a very different character.

For the most part, forces advanced on predictable lines and attempted to grind their way into the target cities. In some cases, this worked, but casualties were high and losses of equipment potentially unsustainable. At the same time, other forms of warfare were intended to break the will of the Ukrainian people. Cyber-attacks attempted to cripple civilian services while missile strikes were directed at the national infrastructure.

In particular, the electricity network was a target. Air defence against missiles and drones became as essential as the capability to disable tanks. The war also had a maritime dimension, albeit a limited one, with Russian control of the Black Sea challenged by land-based missiles.

Equipment

As the conflict continued and losses mounted, both sides required replacements. Ukraine received these from other countries, which created new problems. Personnel had to be trained to use systems they had never encountered before, and often these were supplied in small numbers. Deliveries of Leopard 2 tanks from various nations were agreed upon, necessitating crews to be trained for

Following Ukrainian counterattacks, by October 2022, Russian forces had withdrawn or been pushed back to more defensible positions, although they controlled a large area of territory in the south and east.

In the summer and autumn of 2023 both Russian and Ukrainian forces launched further offensives, but with limited success as the conflict developed into a war of attrition.

them, while others needed to become familiar with the Bradley Infantry Fighting Vehicle (IFV).

In addition to training crews, Ukraine needed to be able to repair and maintain each new weapon system, creating an additional and highly complex logistical problem. Different ammunition was needed for native Ukrainian weapon systems to those supplied by NATO member nations. While this was a better problem to have than lacking weapons, it imposed delays and limitations on deployment.

Russia, on the other hand, started the conflict with vast quantities of hardware in reserve or deployed elsewhere. Overseas sales of Russian weapons and munitions meant that in some cases, stocks existed that could be bought back or supplied as part of an agreement for future sales and assistance. Even so, as

ABOVE: A promotional photograph of a Russian Air Force Sukhoi Su-27 multirole fighter. It is estimated that Russia has more than 300 Su-27s available for active deployment.

BELOW: An M142 HIMARS system launches a rocket in the Donetsk region, May 2023. The high mobility of the system acts as a force-multiplier, enabling a small number of vehicles to greatly influence the course of the war.

ABOVE: **Leopard 1A5 main battle tanks arrive at a military training ground where Ukrainian tank crews are being trained to operate and maintain them by German and Danish military personnel near Klietz, Germany, May 2023.**

BELOW: **A BTR-D armoured personnel carrier. Recognition of friend or foe is always a challenge in combat zones, and even more so where both sides use the same vehicles. The 'Z' identifier, used by Russian forces, became notorious worldwide.**

losses mounted, older equipment was brought out of storage. Expedient equipment, created by mounting whatever weapons were available on any suitable chassis, began to appear as well. As a result, the Russia-Ukraine conflict saw different generations of equipment put into action, as well as hardware from multiple nations. Some deliveries achieved headline status and some weapons became widely

known due to their performance in combat. Yet there was a myriad of other weapons systems in the field, some of them in great numbers, which played their part without receiving much recognition.

Although every effort has been made to include as many weapons types as possible, this book focuses on featuring the main weapons deployed in the Ukraine war.

INFANTRY AND ANTI-PERSONNEL WEAPONS

Small arms and other infantry weapon systems tend not to be glamorized in the way that advanced missiles or highly capable armoured vehicles are. However, they are absolutely vital to the course of any war. The Russian-Ukrainian conflict was characterized by sieges and protracted battles for strong points such as the Azovstal Iron and Steel Works in Mariupol. This was the last point of Ukrainian resistance in the city, surrendering only after a month-long siege.

Cities such as Bakhmut became synonymous with urban combat and sieges. Even where it was possible to send armoured vehicles into an urban area, they required protection from infantry attack. Tanks separated from their infantry supports are highly vulnerable in close terrain, as long experience has shown. At times, small arms were an enabler for anti-tank weapons, clearing infantry supports out of the way. More commonly, they were the tool by which a street or section of a building would be contested.

Ultimately, the conflict revolved around the possession of cities and key points, and that could only be achieved by infantry. Other weapons could interdict supply lines, destroy logistics bases, shoot down aircraft or disable armoured vehicles. Arguably, however, activities were all in support of the final aim – to gain control of the key locations by placing infantry forces in them.

A Ukrainian soldier poses with an AK-74 assault rifle in an entrenched position. Ultimately, the infantry must take and keep possession of objectives. No matter what other weapon systems are present the assault rifle will be the final arbiter of which side attains its objectives.

AK series assault rifles

The AK series of rifles – named after its creator, Anatoly Kalashnikov – began with the AK-47. Both sides fielded large numbers of AK series weapons during the Ukraine conflict.

The AK-47 assault rifle was developed in response to changing needs during World War II. Troops moving in and out of vehicles needed a personal weapon that was shorter and lighter than a traditional long infantry rifle, and urban combat demanded greater firepower. While this could be provided by submachine guns, such weapons lacked range and penetration. The assault rifle was developed as a compromise weapon to meet these new needs.

Chambered for 7.62x39mm (0.3x1.54in) ammunition, the AK-47 was hard to control during full-automatic fire but was otherwise an effective and above all reliable weapon. Development continued, with the AKM emerging in 1959. This was a modernized AK-47, which used stamped instead of machined steel for the receiver. Cheaper to manufacture than the original, the AKM went on to

become the most widely sold – and copied – assault rifle in the world.

AK-74

Lessons learned with the AKM were incorporated into a new version that appeared in 1974. Designated AK-74, this variant was chambered for 5.45x39mm (0.21x1.54in) ammunition. The smaller round offered a higher muzzle velocity – approximately 900m/s (2952ft/s) compared to the 700m/s (2297ft/s) of the AK-47. Precise values can vary according to the condition of the weapon, which in turn affects accuracy. Overall, however, a higher muzzle velocity results in a flatter bullet trajectory and a shorter time for the bullet to reach the target.

There has been much debate over the years concerning the move to smaller calibre ammunition, with critics suggesting the smaller rounds

lack accurate range, penetration and stopping power compared to their predecessors. In an urban engagement, range is rarely a problem other than for marksmen and snipers, but experience in Afghanistan and similar places has exposed a need for long-range accuracy.

However, this is the exception rather than the rule. The AK-74 offered individual infantrymen high-intensity firepower for the suppression or rapid elimination of opponents along with the ability to carry a greater quantity of ammunition. Few engagements take place at more than 300m (984ft) – well inside the AK-74's official effective range of 400–500m (1312–1640ft), particularly in an urban environment.

The move to a smaller calibre was accompanied by other changes. The AK-74 received a redesigned stock, muzzle and gas cylinder. Its weight

AK-74 assault rifle

It is widely claimed the groove in the AK-74's stock was intended to enable the weapon to meet a strict weight limitation. In reality it enables the user to identify the weapon by touch, which is important since the near-identical AKM uses different ammunition.

AK-74 assault rifle
Calibre: 5.45mm (.215in) M74
Operation: Gas
Weight: 3.6kg (7.94lb)
Overall Length: 943mm (37.1in)
Barrel Length: 400mm (15.8in)
Muzzle Velocity: 900m/sec (2952ft/sec)
Feed/Magazine: 30-round detachable box magazine
Range: 300m (984ft)

was significantly reduced from 4.3kg (9.5lb) empty to just over 3kg (6.6lb). Visually, the two are very similar but can be told apart by the muzzle design and grooves along the stock of the AK-74. Magazines are less curved on the AK-74 due to the nature of the ammunition used, along with ridges to allow tactile identification. The magazine and magazine well were designed to be incompatible between the two rifles to prevent attempts to load the wrong ammunition.

The AK-74 has an automatic fire rate of approximately 650 rounds per minute, which is slightly higher than the AK-47's 600. The lighter round used by the AK-74 reduces recoil and improves controllability, though accurate full-automatic fire is not feasible at any significant distance. This is, in theory, not a problem; soldiers can switch to semi-automatic for aimed fire or use the full-auto setting for suppression. However, there is always a tendency to waste ammunition when under stress, especially among troops with insufficient training.

Overall, the AK-74 appears to be an improvement over the equally robust but less controllable AK-47, though it has not been so widely exported. Vast numbers of AK-

47s have been sold worldwide or produced locally. Some of these are licensed versions or new weapons based on the proven AK series; others are unlicensed copies.

On the other hand, the AK-74 has been mostly reserved for use by the Soviet Union and its successors. It was the standard infantry weapon from its introduction and is used to this day by both Russian and Ukrainian forces.

AK-10x series

The AK-10x series was developed from the AKM, with different models featuring slightly different characteristics. All are constructed from advanced materials and have modern features, such as a side rail for mounting a variety of sighting systems and the provision for an under-barrel grenade launcher.

The AK-101, 102 and 108 are chambered for 5.56x45mm (0.22x1.77in) NATO ammunition and are unlikely to be encountered in the Ukraine conflict. The AK-103 is a full-sized assault rifle chambered for 7.62x39mm (0.3x1.54in), while the AK-104 is a carbine variant. The AK-105 is a carbine version of the AK-74. Chambered for the same 5.45x39mm (0.21x1.54in) round, it

AK-12 assault rifle

In 2018, the Russian military began replacing older rifles with the AK-12. The use of Picatinny rails enable sights and other accessories to be quickly swapped as the need arises.

AK-12 assault rifle

Calibre: 7.62mm (.3in)
Operation: Gas
Weight: 3.6kg (7.94lb)
Overall Length: 945mm (37.3in)
Barrel Length: 415mm (16.3in)
Muzzle Velocity: 900m/sec (2952ft/sec)
Feed/Magazine: 30-round detachable box magazine
Range: 500m (1640ft)

is similar in application to the AKS-74U. The AK-107 is also chambered for 5.45mm (0.21in) and incorporates a recoil-damping system as well as a three-round burst mode. At 850–900rpm, the weapon's rate of fire is higher than other AK series weapons. The 7.62x39mm (0.3x1.54in) version is designated AK-109.

The AK-10x series has been exported worldwide but not adopted by the Russian military on a large scale. It is reportedly in use with some law enforcement agencies and units of the Russian armed forces so may be encountered in Ukraine.

Fort-22x series

The Fort-22x series is produced in Ukraine, though it is based on an Israeli weapon.

Ukraine inherited large stocks of AK-74 rifles after the breakup of the Soviet Union, many of which remain in service. Desiring a more modern rifle, Ukraine developed a weapon designated Vulcan or Malyuk. This was a conversion of the AK design to a bullpup configuration. Placing the magazine and feed mechanism behind the trigger assembly moved the point of balance back and allowed a much shorter overall length without reducing barrel length.

Changing the balance point allows a soldier to bring up the muzzle and get the weapon on target more quickly than with a conventionally configured rifle. The difference may be minimal but in urban combat, where encounters can

be sudden and at very close range, it can mean the difference between life and death.

The Vulcan was adopted by the Ukrainian military, though in relatively small numbers, and has seen service with special forces units. It was sufficiently successful that another Bullpup weapon was selected for general issue. That was the Fort-22x series, developed from the Israeli Tavor assault rifle. The Tavor is available in a variety of configurations, a practice that was followed in the design of the Ukrainian version.

The Fort-221 is the standard assault rifle configuration, chambered either for 5.56x45mm (0.22x1.77in) or

5.45x39mm (0.21x1.54in). The Fort-224 is a compact or 'carbine' variant of the same weapon. It can be chambered for either rifle-calibre ammunition or 9x19mm (0.35x0.75in) Luger.

These weapons are produced under licence from Israel Weapon Industries (IWI). Other Israeli weapons, such as the Galil assault rifle and Negev machine gun, have received Ukrainian designations and have seen service in small numbers.

Fort-224

The Fort-224 was adopted for use by the Ukrainian armed forces, and is manufactured domestically. It is derived from the Israeli Tavor assault rifle.

Personal defence weapons

Personal defence weapons (PDWs) are compact and lightweight weapons offering more firepower than a handgun. They are designed to be used in close assaults or by personnel operating in confined spaces, such as vehicle crews.

AKS-74U

Developed in the 1970s and entering service in 1979, the AKS-74U is often described as a submachine gun, challenging the usual assumption that a submachine gun fires pistol-calibre ammunition. It was developed as a self-defence weapon for personnel whose primary task was not engaging the enemy with small arms, such as vehicle crews. However, the weapon was adopted for use in other roles, including law enforcement or urban assault operations. With its stock folded, the AKS-74U is only 490mm (19.3in) long.

The shortened barrel requires a greater twist on the rifling and a modified flash hider, but many components and construction techniques are shared with the AK-74, reducing costs, and function is generally similar. Magazines compatible with the AK-74 can be used, including the standard 30-round and an enlarged 45-round magazine developed for the

AK-74-derived RPK-74 machine gun. Twenty-round magazines are also available but are uncommon.

Ukraine produces the Uzi Pro under licence from Israel Weapon Industries and is developing a similar weapon designated Fort-230. Chambered for 9x19mm (0.35x0.75in), the Fort-230 has a telescoping stock and folding foregrip.

HANDGUNS

Handguns are, for the most part, last-ditch self-defence weapons. They have traditionally been carried by pilots or other personnel who do not intend to come into direct contact with the enemy or as an emergency backup for combat personnel and are not considered 'combat' weapons. However, in the Russia-Ukraine conflict there has been significant urban and trench combat. A handgun can be effective in such extreme close-quarters situations.

The primary Russian service handgun is the Makarov, which is chambered for 9x18mm Makarov ammunition. In service since the 1950s, this weapon was intended to be replaced but has remained ubiquitous due to financial issues and difficulties with newer weapons. The replacement weapon was to be the MP-443 Grach, which is compatible with NATO 9x19mm ammunition.

Ukraine inherited a very large amount of small arms from the Soviet Union. In addition to the Soviet-era handguns found among this legacy arsenal, such as the TT-33 Tokarev, Ukraine has received shipments of weapons from overseas. These include Czech Cz-75 and Cz-82 pistols, and Glock and Beretta handguns donated by Canada and the USA.

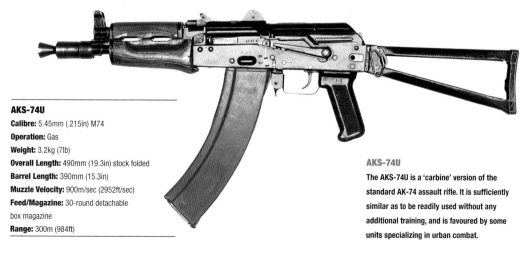

AKS-74U

Calibre: 5.45mm (.215in) M74
Operation: Gas
Weight: 3.2kg (7lb)
Overall Length: 490mm (19.3in) stock folded
Barrel Length: 390mm (15.3in)
Muzzle Velocity: 900m/sec (2952ft/sec)
Feed/Magazine: 30-round detachable box magazine
Range: 300m (984ft)

AKS-74U

The AKS-74U is a 'carbine' version of the standard AK-74 assault rifle. It is sufficiently similar as to be readily used without any additional training, and is favoured by some units specializing in urban combat.

Marksman rifles

Relatively small-calibre weapons increase the firepower of individual soldiers and therefore the capability of the unit to suppress enemy forces. However, larger-calibre weapons are generally preferred for precision at longer ranges.

Dragunov SVD-S

The iconic wooden furniture of the SVD rifle has been replaced by modern materials but its function remains the same; to provide accurate and precise fire beyond the range attainable by assault rifles.

Not all of those who are armed with such weapons are snipers; that designation is reserved for soldiers who have undertaken extensive training in observation and concealment as well as marksmanship. Designated marksmen are trained to shoot to a comparable standard without requiring the rare talent to become a fully qualified sniper.

Dragunov SVD

The Dragunov SVD, developed from the AK assault rifle, was developed from the late 1950s to the 1960s and might be more properly considered a marksman rifle rather than a sniping weapon. It is accurate to 800m (2625ft), which is entirely adequate for most engagements, but lacks the precision at longer ranges for true sniping work. On the other hand, the SVD is relatively cheap to produce. Newer versions feature modern materials rather than the wooden furniture of the originals.

The Dragunov SVD has found considerable export success and has been widely copied.

Zabroyar Z-10

Ukraine also fields a marksman rifle developed from an earlier weapon system – in this case the Armalite AR-10.

Dragunov SVD-S
Calibre: 7.62mm (.3in)
Operation: Gas, rotating bolt
Weight: 4.68kg (10.3lb)
Overall Length: 1225mm (48.2in)
Barrel Length: 560mm (22.2in)
Muzzle Velocity: 830m/sec (2723ft/sec)
Feed/Magazine: 10-round detachable box magazine
Range: 800m (2625ft)

Zabroyar Z-10

Armed with a Z-10 marksman rifle, a Ukrainian sniper with the 28th Brigade looks towards a Russian position from a frontline trench near Bakhmut, Ukraine, March 2023.

Designated Zabroyar Z-10, this weapon is in use with special operations units and may be more widely issued over time. It is chambered for 7.62x51mm (0.3x2.01in) ammunition fed from a 10- or 20-round magazine. As with many other modern rifles, the Z-10 can accept a range of accessories, including optical or thermal sighting aids fixed to its mounting rail, and can be fitted with a suppressor.

Sniping and anti-materiel weapons

For sniping at long ranges, bolt-action weapons are generally preferred. On average, a bolt-action weapon will be slightly more accurate than a semi-automatic one.

This is true for various reasons. In a semi-automatic weapon, some propellant gas is taken off to work the action, potentially causing inconsistencies that might not matter at 200m (656ft) but become significant at longer ranges. Likewise, fewer moving parts in a bolt-action weapon means less to affect the weapon alignment as the bullet travels down the barrel. Most shooters would not notice any difference, but snipers are trained to shoot at extreme ranges.

Stalingrad

The Russian military fields the Lobayev TVSL-8 Stalingrad chambered for 8.59mm (0.338in) Lapua Magnum or 7.62mm (.3in) Winchester Magnum. These powerful, heavy rounds are reportedly accurate to over 1.6km (1 mile). For even longer-range sniping, specialist weapons are required.

Lobayev Arms produces the SVLK-14S Twilight, which is reportedly capable of accurate fire from 2.5km (1.6 miles) and possibly further. It is chambered for 10.36mm (0.408in) or 9.53mm (0.375in) Cheyenne Tactical ammunition. It has been claimed that Russian snipers have made extreme long-range shots using Lobayev rifles, though these weapons are not officially in service.

Alligator

The Ukrainian armed forces adopted the Snipex Alligator in 2021. Chambered in 14.5x11mm (0.57x0.43in), this anti-materiel rifle is capable of destroying equipment or penetrating lightly armoured vehicles

Alligator anti-materiel rifle
The Snipex Alligator is a highly powerful weapon, with an effective firing range of 2000m (6600ft), putting it in the same category as the Barrett M82.

and can be used for long-range sniping. Its effective range is around 2km (1.2 miles), but its projectile will travel more than three times that far. Weapons this powerful are heavy and require specialist configuration to absorb their ferocious recoil. The large muzzle brake and padded shoulder rest are assisted by a recoil isolator, but the weapon must still be carefully positioned and supported. The Snipex T-Rex, a bullpup-configuration single-shot weapon, is also in use.

Snipex Alligator
Calibre: 14.5×11mm
Operation: Recoil-operated rotating bolt
Weight: 25kg (55lb)
Overall Length: 2000mm (79in)
Barrel Length: 1200mm (47in)
Muzzle Velocity: 980m/s (3,200ft/s)
Feed/Magazine: 5-round detachable box magazine
Range: 2000m (6600ft)

Machine guns and squad support weapons

All militaries agree that it is beneficial to have heavy automatic firepower available at a small-unit level, though preferences vary as to how to provide it.

A squad support weapon may essentially be an overgrown rifle with a heavier barrel and greater ammunition capacity. This has the advantage that any soldier can take over the support weapon as required and without any additional training. However, heat build-up can be a problem.

If a true machine gun rather than a rifle variant is used, there are still questions to be answered. Using a weapon chambered for the same round as the infantry rifle simplifies logistics and allows more ammunition to be carried, but assault rifle-calibre machine guns do not have the same penetration and destructive power as those chambered for a heavier round. They do have the advantage of a quickly detachable barrel, allowing one barrel to cool while another is in use. This preserves accuracy, reduces malfunctions and prolongs the life of the weapon.

RPK

Russian forces make extensive use of the RPK, which is designated a light machine gun but is an upscaled AK assault rifle. Capable of using AK rifle magazines or a 75-round drum, the RPK is a versatile weapon chambered for 7.62x39mm (0.3x1.54in) ammunition. It weighs 4.8kg (10.6lb) empty, compared to 3kg (6.6lb) for a 5.45mm (0.21in) AK-74 assault rifle. A more modern but similar weapon is the RPK-74, which is to the AK-74 as the RPK is to the AKM. It is chambered for the same ammunition – 5.45x39mm (0.21x1.54in) – as infantry rifles. While folding-stock variants of both weapons are available, the upgraded RPK-74M is only available with a folding stock.

DP-28/DPM

The DP machine gun (variously designated DP-27 or DP-28) was developed in the 1920s and went

RPK-74 light support weapon
Calibre: 5.45mm (.21in) M74
Operation: Gas, air-cooled
Weight: 9kg (19.84lb)
Overall Length: 1160mm (45.67in)
Barrel Length: 658mm (25.9in)
Muzzle Velocity: 800m/sec (2600ft/sec)
Feed/Magazine: 30- or 45-round detachable box magazine
Range: 1000m (3280ft) +

RPK-74 light support weapon

The RPK-74 is a rifle-type squad support weapon. It has the advantage of ammunition and magazine commonality with other members of the unit, but heat build-up is a problem under sustained fire.

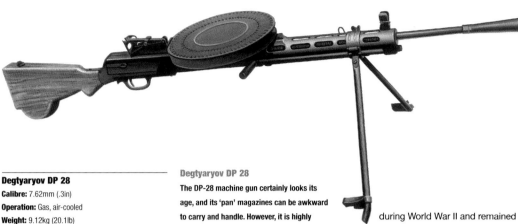

Degtyaryov DP 28

Calibre: 7.62mm (.3in)
Operation: Gas, air-cooled
Weight: 9.12kg (20.1lb)
Overall Length: 1290mm (50.8in)
Barrel Length: 605mm (23.8in))
Muzzle Velocity: 840m/sec (2756ft/sec)
Feed/Magazine: 47-round pan magazine
Cyclic Rate: 475rpm
Range: 800m (2624ft)

Vintage machine gun

A Ukrainian volunteer mans a mounted DP machine gun. The weapon's unusual downward ejection system is one of its many unique features.

Degtyaryov DP 28

The DP-28 machine gun certainly looks its age, and its 'pan' magazines can be awkward to carry and handle. However, it is highly reliable and has a solid record in combat. With large numbers in storage it may yet return to widespread front-line service.

into service with Soviet forces in 1928. Chambered for 7.62x54mm (0.3x2.13in), it was fed from a distinctive pan magazine atop the weapon and used by infantry and to arm some vehicles. An updated version designated DPM appeared during World War II and remained in service until replaced by the RPK. Although officially replaced, older weapons have remained in service or been broken out of storage with the progression of the conflict.

Despite the limitations imposed by its 47-round magazine and the awkwardness caused by its weight atop the weapon, the DPM proved reliable and acceptably effective. Large numbers were manufactured, and some examples

PKP Pecheneg light support weapon

Calibre: 7.62mm (.3in)
Operation: Gas
Weight: 8.7kg (19.18lb)
Overall Length: 1155mm (45.47in)
Barrel Length: 640mm (25.19in)
Muzzle Velocity: 825m/sec (2706ft/sec)
Feed/Magazine: 100- and 200-round belt-fed magazine
Range: 1500m (4921ft)

PKP Pecheneg light support weapon

Although an improvement on the PKM it was intended to replace, the PKP was introduced slowly due to budget restrictions. Variants include bullpup-configuration versions and a short-barrelled weapon for use by special forces.

PKM general purpose machine gun

The PKM was developed by Mikhail Kalashnikov and uses 7.62x54mm ammunition that is not compatible with the assault rifles it supports. This perhaps makes it more useful as a mounted weapon than in the squad support role.

PKM general purpose machine gun

Calibre: 7.62mm (.3in) M1943
Operation: Gas, air-cooled
Weight: 9kg (19.84lb)
Overall Length: 1160mm (45.67in)
Barrel Length: 658mm (25.9in)
Muzzle Velocity: 800m/sec (2600ft/sec)
Feed/Magazine: Belt-fed (belts contained in boxes)
Range: 710rpm

were in service with Ukrainian forces at the time of the Russian invasion. It is possible that as the conflict goes on, more will be broken out of storage.

PK/PKM/PKP

The PK was developed as a replacement for the DP and was introduced in 1961. It is a more conventional, belt-fed, 7.62x54mm (0.3x2.13in) weapon designed for infantry use as well as vehicle mounting. In due course, an updated version designated PKM entered production and was adopted for service with Soviet forces in 1969. This was further updated into the PKP Pecheneg general purpose machine gun. With better cooling and

the ability to be fitted with telescopic sights, the PKP is currently in service with some Russian formations, including special forces.

DShK

This machine gun was developed in the 1930s and adopted by the Soviet Union at the end of that decade. The DShK is chambered for 12.7x108mm (0.5x4.25in) ammunition. During World War II, it saw service as an infantry support and anti-aircraft weapon and was also mounted on tanks and other vehicles. It was produced until 1980 and sold widely overseas. Although the NSV heavy machine gun was introduced as a replacement in the 1970s, the DShK continues to see service alongside it.

PKM in action

A Ukrainian soldier aims a PK machine gun in the newly liberated village of Neskuchne, Ukraine, June 2023.

INFANTRY ANTI-ARMOUR WEAPONS

The Soviet-era Red Army considered anti-tank weapons to be the most important weapons of all. Armoured vehicles were created to smash through defences that would easily repel an infantry assault, and while the best counter to a tank is widely considered to be another tank, the ability of infantry to defend themselves against armoured assault is vital.

Infantry anti-tank weapons allow a stand-off attack to be made from a position of cover or concealment. The heavier versions can be considered entirely defensive as they cannot be repositioned quickly unless provided with a vehicle mount. On the other hand, they do permit engagements at longer ranges, covering a wider area in return for reduced mobility.

Man-portable weapons are generally less potent and have a shorter range but are in many ways more flexible. The lightest man-portable anti-tank weapons are typically of marginal effectiveness against a main battle tank. Heavier versions are a threat to any armoured vehicle and typically have guidance systems, whereas smaller weapons do not.

The usual mode of attack for infantry anti-armour weapons is a shaped charge. This uses explosives to create a jet of superheated gas, or plasma, which burns through armour rather than blasting it apart like a conventional explosive warhead would.

The RPG-7 and its derivatives provide infantry with a measure of anti-tank capability, though effectiveness is marginal against front-line tanks. The ability to engage bunkers and fortified positions is equally important.

Disposable anti-armour weapons

Some of the earliest non-reusable infantry anti-tank weapons were hand-thrown grenades. Using a parachute or streamer to align the weapon in flight made a shaped charge feasible, though a very close approach was needed.

Despite the drawbacks of these weapons, they remained in production into the Cold War era when the last example, the RKG-3, was earmarked to be replaced with a more advanced weapon designated RPG-18.

RPG-18

The RPG-18 offers, in theory at least, a basic anti-armour capability without overburdening the user. It consists of a disposable launch tube with a flip-up sight, delivering a 64mm (2.52in) High-Explosive Anti-Tank shaped-charge warhead out to about 200m (656ft). The weapon's nickname, Mukha, or 'Fly' is apt; its warhead is incapable

of seriously harming a main battle tank but may be effective against lighter vehicles.

The main advantage of the RPG-18 over the RPG-7 family is its relative lightness at 2.6kg (5.7lb) as opposed to 7kg (15.4lb) and ease of carry. Once used, it is discarded. However, the RPG-7 family can be used to attack bunkers and infantry positions whereas the RPG-18's very small blast radius makes it useful only as an anti-vehicle weapon.

RPG-26

The RPG-26 is a significant improvement on its predecessor.

In service since 1985, it is a similar weapon but uses a 72.5mm (2.83in) diameter warhead. Its effective range is longer, at about 250m (820ft), and it is useful against buildings and other structures as well as vehicles. A heavier variant designated RShG-2 with a thermobaric warhead is available, intended for use against enemy-held buildings and positions.

RPG-27

A larger version of the RPG-26, developed in the 1980s, the RPG-27 launches a 105mm (4.13in) warhead which was designed to keep pace with advances in vehicle armour emerging

RPG-26

Calibre: 72.5mm (2.83in)
Operation: Rocket motor
Weight: 2.9kg (6.4lb) (loaded)
Overall Length: 770mm (30in)
Muzzle Velocity: 144m/s (470ft/sec)
Feed/Magazine: Single-shot, muzzle-loaded
Range: 250m (820ft)

RPG-26

The RPG-18 and 26 family of weapons are disposable and therefore are provided only with the most basic of sights. The original RPG-18 was effective only against armoured vehicles but more recent versions have a variety of applications.

RPG-27

Even disposable weapons have become increasingly sophisticated. The RPG-27 uses a precursor charge that works on the same principle of the explosive reactive armour (ERA) it is intended to defeat. Its explosion disrupts the blast from the ERA, preventing it from disrupting the main charge.

RPG-27

Calibre: 105mm (4.13in)
Operation: Rocket motor
Weight: 7.6kg (17lb) (loaded)
Overall Length: 1155mm (45.47in)
Muzzle Velocity: 120m/s (390ft/s)
Feed/Magazine: Single-shot, muzzle-loaded
Range: 200m (660ft)

around that time. The standard warhead uses a precursor charge to disrupt explosive reactive armour and can penetrate 600mm (23.62in) of rolled steel even after encountering ERA. Penetration is around 750mm (29.53in) of unprotected steel or 1.5m (4.9ft) of reinforced concrete. The RShG-1 variant is very similar but uses a thermobaric warhead. In 2011 another variant, designated RMG, came into service. Its tandem warhead offers superior penetration of ERA and enhanced effect against bunkers and personnel targets.

Firing an RPG-27 can be rather obvious, with a 27m (89ft) backblast area in which a large cloud of dust and debris is thrown up. The launcher component is constructed from aluminium covered in fibreglass, and is intended like other weapons of the type to be discarded after use.

With only a basic flip-up sight and no capacity to use more advanced sighting systems, effective range is

limited to about 200m (656ft) as with most similar weapons. The RPG-27 is sometimes referred to as Tavolga, or Meadow Grass.

Further developments
Development of the RPG-27 family continued with the 125mm (4.92in) RPG-28, whose tandem warhead is the most potent in the whole weapon family. The RPG-30, entering Russian service in 2012, has a precursor rocket to trigger active defence systems, leaving the main projectile unharmed.

Many NATO standard anti-armour weapons have also been supplied to the Ukrainian armed forces, including the M72 light anti-tank weapon (LAW) and NLAW.

M72 LAW
The M72 Light Anti-tank Weapon launches a 66mm (2.6in) projectile from a disposable tube with basic flip-up sights. It can engage a tank-

sized target out to 250m (820ft) or so with reasonable accuracy, and can penetrate 200mm (9in) of steel armour. These weapons were produced in huge numbers, and while they are overshadowed by more modern anti-armour systems, they remain extremely effective against lighter armoured vehicles and dug-in positions. Drone-mounted variants are currently under development.

NLAW
The Next-Generation Light Anti-tank Weapon (NLAW) has a maximum range of 800m (2624ft) and can be set for either top-attack or direct-fire modes, depending on the target. Guidance is automatic, using predicted-line-of-sight with the projectile flying 1m (3ft) above the direct path to the target.

Engagement time is very short, and the weapon can be fired from as close as 20m (65ft). The shaped-charge warhead can defeat 500mm (19in) of steel armour.

RPG-7

Arguably the simplest non-disposable anti-armour weapon available, the RPG-7 was developed from World War II weaponry and has the same purpose: to deliver an unguided shaped-charge warhead over a modest distance.

The RPG is of marginal effectiveness against main battle tanks but can eliminate lighter vehicles and positions of cover and can pose a threat to helicopters or even low-flying aircraft.

The original weapon of this type was the Panzerfaust, a World War II German expedient designed to take on enemy tanks at close range. From this concept, the Soviet Union developed the RPG-1, which proved to be a disappointment. It was developed into a more effective weapon designated RPG-2, which entered service in 1949. By this time, the weapon was already incapable of defeating the new generation of tanks. This, combined with a combat range of about 100m (328ft) against mobile targets, made it clear that something better was required.

Entering service in 1961, the RPG-7 was a refinement of the earlier models using the same basic principles. The reusable component of the weapon is a tube with hand grips and a basic sight, into which the rear of a rocket-propelled grenade is inserted. This arrangement is known as a spigot mortar. The weapon is recoilless, in that the projectile is self-propelled and accelerates once it has left the weapon. However, it does create a backblast, which can throw up dust and debris to give away the launcher's position. This may also pose problems if operating

RPG-7D

Calibre: 40mm (1.57in)
Operation: Rocket motor
Weight: 7kg (15lb)
Overall Length: 950mm (37.4in)
Muzzle Velocity: 115m/sec (377ft/sec)
Feed/Magazine: Single-shot, muzzle-loaded
Range: 920m (3018ft)

RPG-7D

The RPG-7 series of weapons has been upgraded over the years, mainly in the form of improved sighting systems and variant warheads. It remains a relatively cheap and simple way to get a warhead to the target.

the weapon in a confined space or with friendly personnel close behind. Official sources state that only 2m (6.56ft) clearance behind the weapon is necessary, but exactly what is meant by 'necessary' is an open question.

The RPG-7 has a theoretical maximum range of about 920m (3018ft), after which the warhead self-detonates. In reality, there is a reasonable chance of hitting a static target such as a building at up to 500m (1640ft), while even a slowly moving tank is unlikely to be hit beyond 200m (656ft). Wind conditions play a large part in this; the guidance fins on a projectile are at the very rear, causing the weapon to turn into a crosswind. Even in calm conditions, precise targeting of weak spots is not possible with an unguided weapon. This is offset by the fact that the weapon is cheap and can be deployed in large numbers. All projectiles fit the 40mm (1.57in) diameter launch tube, but their physical characteristics vary. The basic warhead is designated PG-7V. It has a diameter of 85mm (3.35in) and uses a shaped charge to potentially penetrate 260mm (10.24in) of rolled steel armour. The PG-7VM is an updated version. Its smaller diameter of 70mm (2.76in) makes it less susceptible to wind effects, while armour penetration is increased to 300mm (11.81in). The 73mm (2.87in) diameter PG-7VS increases penetration to 400m (1312ft), whilst its cheaper PG-7VS1 variant has a reduced performance.

The most potent anti-tank warhead is designated PG-7VL. Its 93mm (3.66in) casing permits a greater charge capable of penetrating 500mm (19.6in) of conventional armour. However, these are all conventional shaped-charge HEAT (High Explosive

A Ukrainian soldier fires an RPG-7 during training in the Donetsk region, May 2023.

Anti-Tank) warheads, which are less effective against explosive reactive armour. The PG-7VR variant, utilizing a 105mm (4.13in) casing, uses a tandem warhead to defeat reactive armour. It is rated at 600m (1968ft) against ERA and 750m (2460ft) against conventional steel.

The RPG-7 can also launch a 40mm (1.57in) anti-personnel projectile and a 105mm (4.13in) thermobaric warhead designated TBG-7V. Thermobaric weapons use a combination of explosive vapour and oxygen from the surrounding air to create huge pressures and temperatures, earning them the name 'fuel-air weapons'. Thermobaric warheads are particularly deadly against personnel in confined spaces but can also damage vehicles and equipment.

Other reloadable anti-armour weapons

Reloadable anti-armour weapons are more expensive to produce than disposable systems and are overall heavier. They typically require specialist training rather than being intended for use by an ordinary infantry soldier.

Most reloadable anti-armour weapons are unguided, though with a greater effective range than their disposable equivalents. Guided shoulder-launched Man-Portable Anti-Tank Systems (MANPATS) are more complex and expensive but have demonstrated their worth against even front-line tanks.

RPG-29 Vampir

The RPG-29 consists of a reusable tube with a pistol grip and sighting system. This is usually a 2.7x magnification

RPG-32

The RPG-32 can launch five different projectiles, of either 105mm (4.13in) or 72mm (2.83in) diameter. All have similar ballistic performance, requiring no adjustments to the sights.

optical sight but a night sight is also available. The reusable component weighs 27kg (59.5lb), much more than an RPG-7 or similar weapon, but performance is accordingly greater. Where an RPG-7 is a marginal threat to main battle tank the RPG-29 has proven effective in disabling the most modern armoured vehicles.

Three primary warheads can be launched, out to a maximum distance of about 1600m (5249ft). The PG29V warhead uses a tandem charge to defeat explosive reactive armour, while the TBG-29V is a thermobaric weapon intended for use against personnel or infantry-occupied structures. The OG-29 warhead offers more conventional high explosive/fragmentation capability

against infantry. Since the projectile is unguided, accuracy at long range is questionable even if the user is accustomed to the weapon's significant recoil. The reason for this recoil is that the projectile burns all its propellant in the tube, accelerating very rapidly during this period. This means the RPG-29 cannot be tracked back to its launch position by a smoke trail, unlike other shoulder-fired rocket weapons.

RPG-32

A reloadable launcher developed from the RPG-27 family, the RPG-32 uses a 105mm (4.13in) warhead. It was developed for export to Jordan but is also in use with the Russian armed forces.

Panzerfaust 3

One advantage of spigot mortar type launchers such as Panzerfaust 3 is that only the rear section of the projectile needs to fit the tube. This makes it possible to use a variety of different munitions from the same launcher.

Panzerfaust 3

Calibre: 60mm (2.4in) barrel, 110mm (4.3in) warhead
Overall Length: 950mm (37.4in)
Muzzle velocity: 115.0 m/s (377 ft/s)
Weight (unloaded): 2.3kg (5lb 1oz)
Warhead weight (bunker busting): 13.3kg (29lb 5oz)
Range: c.920m (3018ft)
Sights: UP-7V Telescopic sight

Panzerfaust 3

Panzerfaust 3 is a NATO weapon supplied to the Ukrainian armed forces. It consists of a reusable launch tube with a 60mm (2.36in) diameter, into which the rear section of the 110mm (4.33in) projectile is inserted. It is effective to 300m (984ft) against a moving target and 400m (1312ft) against structures or static vehicles. The standard High-Explosive Anti-Tank (HEAT) warhead can penetrate 400mm (15.75in) of rolled steel armour, with the Pzf 3-T version's tandem warhead penetrating up to 700mm (27.56in). An improved tandem warhead (Pzf 3-IT) uses a standoff probe and High-Explosive Squash Head tandem warheads to defeat explosive reactive armour more effectively. There are also anti-bunker (Bunkerfaust), fragmentation and smoke variants, and improved sighting systems are also available. It is not clear which of these, were supplied to Ukraine.

CARL GUSTAV RECOILLESS RIFLE

The Carl Gustav is an 84mm (3.3in) recoilless rifle, capable of delivering a variety of munitions. In addition to anti-armour projectiles, smoke and illuminating rounds are available as well as anti-personnel flechette ammunition. Modern versions are far more advanced than the original unguided weapon, featuring a laser rangefinder which can be used to deliver pre-programmed airbursts over enemy positions. Some munitions can be set for direct attack or a delayed detonation, which allows penetration of walls and other cover.

Carl Gustav recoilless rifle

Calibre: 84mm (3.31in)
Overall Length: 1130mm (44in)
Muzzle velocity: 230–255m/s (750–840ft/s)
Weight (unloaded): 14.2kg (31lb)
Rate of fire: 6 rounds per minute
Range: 500m (1600ft) against stationary vehicles; 2000m (6600ft) using rocket-boosted laser-guided ammunition

Anti-tank guided missile systems

Guided missile systems are typically more powerful and have a longer range than Man-Portable Anti-Tank Systems (MANPATS). Most are mounted on vehicles or helicopters, enabling a relatively light platform to endanger tanks.

Such weapons are best used from ambush, firing into the flanks or rear of an enemy formation. If used from a ground mount, guided missiles systems can be concealed more easily but are not capable of a rapid retirement in the face of return fire unless the launcher is abandoned by its crew.

Soviet-era ATGMs

Adopted by the Red Army in 1970, the 9K111 Fagot ('bassoon') is a wire-guided anti-tank missile using semi-active command line of sight (SACLOS). Essentially this means the weapon is automatically guided to the aim point; so long as the operator keeps the weapon's sight aligned with the target it will be hit. However,

experience has shown that the backblast of the weapon makes the launch point easy to spot and return fire that causes an operator to flinch can be effective in disrupting an attack. The 9K111 and its variants were designed to minimize this problem by allowing the crew to remain behind cover. Large numbers were inherited by the Russian and Ukrainian armed forces at the breakup of the Soviet Union.

9K111 Fagot

The 9K111 was the first SACLOS weapon in the Soviet arsenal. It has a range of 2000m (6600ft), though its claimed 80–90 per cent hit rate diminishes at greater distances. The launcher is mounted on a collapsible

9K111 Fagot

A Ukrainian soldier fires an 9K111 Fagot anti-tank missile during training near Chasiv Yar, Donetsk Oblast, as the Russia-Ukraine war continues, August 2023.

tripod and can be dismantled for infantry transportation. The original missile can penetrate 400mm (15.8in) of armour if striking at a good angle, but this is greatly diminished as the angle increases.

More advanced missiles offered better performance. The 9M111-2 has a more powerful tandem warhead with a penetration of 460mm (18.11in) through ERA. 9K111M added thermal sights to the launcher and increases in both range and penetration.

9K113 Konkurs

Larger and more effective than the 9K111, the 9K113 Konkurs ('competition') can be used from the same ground launcher as the 9K111 but primarily is mounted on vehicles. It arms the BMP-2 as well as the BDRM-2 reconnaissance vehicle, giving infantry and light armoured forces a measure of anti-tank capability.

Penetration is stated as 600–670mm (23.62–26.38in) of armour out to a distance of 4km (2.5 miles). This is achieved by using a larger missile than the 9K111, at 135mm (5.31in) diameter.

The 9K113 trades high-end capability for cost-effectiveness, in keeping with the doctrine that more adequate weapon systems are better than not enough extremely good ones. The missile velocity is relatively low as a result.

However, the improved Konkurs-M tandem warhead can endanger even the most modern tanks.

FGM-148 Javelin

It may be that history records the HIMARS artillery system as the star of the show in the Ukraine-Russia conflict, but even so, the Javelin deserves an honourable mention.

One of the earliest NATO weapons sent to Ukraine, Javelin was instrumental in blunting the first armoured assaults and inflicting heavy casualties throughout the conflict. This in turn allowed Ukraine to demonstrate it could survive and was therefore worth supporting.

Entering US service in 1996, the FGM-148 Javelin was developed in response to a need for a portable guided anti-armour weapon to replace

the M47 Dragon. The reusable component is known as the command launch unit, or CLU, and is equipped with 4x optical sights for use in daylight. The night sight component has selectable 4x/7x magnification

FGM-148 Javelin

By blunting the initial Russian armoured advances, weapons like Javelin demonstrated to other nations that supporting Ukraine was worthwhile.

FGM-148 Javelin

Configuration: two-stage, solid fuel
Deployment: man-portable
Length: 1.1m (43in)
Diameter: 127mm (5in)
Launch weight: 22.1kg (48.7lb)
Range: 2500m (8200ft)
Rate of fire: 3 rounds in 2 minutes

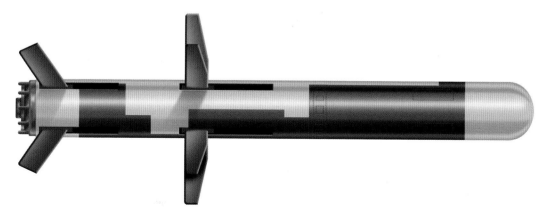

and can be used for surveillance as well as targeting. The CLU is 1.2m (3.9ft) long and weighs 6.4kg (14lb) unloaded. It is normally fired from the shoulder but can be mounted on a vehicle.

The projectile carries an 8.4kg (18.5lb) warhead, bringing the loaded weight of the weapon to 22.1kg (48.7lb). The projectile is soft-launched, engaging its rocket propulsion once clear of the weapon. This reduces recoil and backblast,

enabling Javelin to be launched from confined spaces and reducing the chance a launch point will be spotted. Effective range is given as 2500m (8200ft), but it is claimed that Javelin can perform out to 4000m (13,123ft).

Guidance uses passive infrared, making Javelin a 'fire and forget' weapon. This is a great improvement on previous wire-guided weapons such as the M47 Dragon, which required the user to remain exposed to return fire while guiding the weapon. Two

attack modes are available; direct fire can be used against anything from a bunker to a helicopter, while top attack aims to defeat a tank's protection by striking its weaker upper surfaces. The penetration of the tandem HEAT warhead is classified but is stated as sufficient to defeat 750mm (29.53in) or more of steel armour. Experience in Ukrainian hands has demonstrated Javelin's effectiveness, to the point where images of 'Saint Javelin' have become popular.

Firing practice
A Ukrainian soldier training with the FGM-148 Javelin system. The weapon's indirect trajectory facilitates an attack against the relative weak top of a tank or other armoured vehicle.

Skif/Shershen

The Skif ATGM was developed in the 2000s for the Ukrainian armed forces and adopted in 2011. Although it resembles Russian weapons such as the 9K113, it is a new system.

Originally delivered in small numbers it was also offered for export. Stocks intended for overseas customers were redirected at the outbreak of the conflict. They proved effective in the early weeks of the Russian invasion, as did the man-portable Stunga-P which was introduced at the same time.

The Skif can launch either 130mm (5.12in) or 152mm (5.98in) missiles, each with anti-armour and anti-personnel variants. The 130mm (5.12in) RK-2S uses a tandem-warhead HEAT warhead, with the RK2OF high-explosive/fragmentation missile for use against personnel and lightly protected targets. The 152mm (5.98in) RK-2M-K is stated to be capable of penetrating 1100mm (43.31in) of armour even through ERA. The RK-2M-OF HE/Fragmentation warhead is the associated light armour/anti-personnel munition.

Belarussian version

The Belarussian version of Skif is designated Shershen ('Hornet') and is similar in most ways. It shares the same impressive performance characteristics and can be set to automatically seek the target or follow a weather-resistant laser. The Shershen missile flies several metres above the laser beam, descending to make its attack. It is credited with a maximum range of 7500m (24,606ft). As with similar weapon systems, Shershen can be mounted on vehicles. Shershen-D uses two missiles mounted side by side, while Shershen-Q and Shershen-M mount four missiles.

Skif ATGM

A Skif simulator on display at the Weapons and Security-2021 exhibition in Kyiv.

MILAN

The European MILAN missile system has been widely exported since its introduction in 1972. It has seen service with the Ukrainian forces since 2022.

MILAN began as a joint French/German project in the 1960s, quickly establishing itself as a highly effective anti-tank weapon. It is primarily used from a ground mount, though it can arm vehicles. The firing post consists of a tripod and optical sensor, with the launch tube carried separately and the weapon assembled once in position. Ukrainian forces have compared using the MILAN system to sniper work; firing from a position of concealment when a suitable target presents itself.

MILAN 2

In 1984, the improved MILAN 2 system entered service, increasing armour penetration from 350mm (13.78in) to 550mm (21.65in). This was achieved by enlarging the missile, from 103mm (4.06in) diameter to 115mm (4.53in). MILAN 2T uses a tandem warhead for further increased penetration – 880mm (34.65in) after penetrating ERA. MILAN 3 entered service in 1996, increasing missile size again to 125mm (4.92in) and adding an infrared guidance system.

The optical sights of earlier versions were enhanced with a thermal system on the lightweight MILAN ADT, which also features integrated thermal and optical sights. This variant appeared in 2006. The latest update is MILAN ER (extended range) which increases the weapon's range to 3km (1.9 miles) and penetration to 1000mm (39.37in) of armour behind ERA. Most components of earlier MILAN systems are compatible with the new version, and with huge numbers sold worldwide spares should not be difficult to come by.

MILAN 3

Configuration: two-stage, solid fuel
Deployment: man-portable
Length: 1.2m (3ft 1in)
Diameter: 0.115m (4.5in)
Weight: 16.4kg (36lb)
Range: 200–2000m (660–6560ft); 3000m (MILAN ER)
Rate of fire: 3 rounds in 2 minutes
Warhead: solid-fuel rocket; single or tandem HEAT

MILAN 3

MILAN is a well proven system that has been upgraded several times. All older firing posts can be brought up to MILAN 3 standards, which permits the use of all current MILAN munitions.

BGM-71 TOW

The BGM-71 TOW missile system dates from the 1970s and has proven itself effective in conflicts in Asia and the Middle East. It can be deployed in a ground mount or aboard a variety of vehicles.

BGM-71 TOW

The BGM-71 TOW missile system can be mounted on a variety of light vehicles, creating highly mobile tank destroyers. The most recent versions retain wire-guidance capability, which cannot be jammed nor even detected by its emissions.

BGM-71 TOW

Configuration: two-stage, solid fuel
Deployment: man-portable
Length: 1.51m (4ft 11in)
Diameter: 152mm (6in)
Weight (warhead): 3.9–6.14kg (8.6–13.5lb)
Range: 3750m (2.3 miles)
Guidance system: Optically tracked, wire-guided (wireless radio-guided in RF variants)

The BGM-71 Tube-launched, Optically tracked, Wire-guided (TOW) missile was developed in the 1960s and entered service in 1970. It is wire-guided, requiring the user to keep the target in the sights until impact. The original missiles were rated as penetrating 500mm (19.6in) of armour, though recent studies suggest performance was a little less than this.

The original BGM-71A model was followed by BGM-71B, increasing missile speed and range from 3000–3750m (9842–12,303ft).

ITOW (Improved TOW), also designated BGM-71C, arrived in 1976, adding a probe to ensure the correct detonation distance and improving penetration to 630mm (24.8in) of armour. This in turn was followed by TOW2 in 1983, which can launch earlier missiles but is lighter and has better guidance. Penetration increased to 900mm (35.43in) of armour.

TOW 2A, also known as BGM-71E, was introduced in 1987. Its tandem warhead is rated at penetrating 900mm (35.43in) of armour behind

ERA. TOW 2A also introduced dual-mode guidance. Missiles can be guided wirelessly but retain wire-guidance capability for use where jamming or interference is expected. The 1987 TOW 2B is a top-attack variant. Extended-range and anti-bunker variants are also available.

TOW systems are standard armament on M2 and M3 infantry fighting vehicles (IFVs), which have been supplied to Ukraine. The launcher can also be fitted to lighter vehicles, making some expedient conversions a possibility.

ARMOURED FIGHTING VEHICLES

A successful armoured vehicle must balance mobility against protection and capability. For an armoured fighting vehicle (AFV), this is straight combat power; the ability to destroy other armoured vehicles and to smash fortified positions. At the outset of the conflict, it would have been reasonable to expect sweeping Russian advances spearheaded by tank units. For many years Soviet (and Russian) tank design philosophy was geared to such operations, with features such as a low silhouette and rounded turrets increasing survivability in a fluid battle space. Western designs were more defensive, with a higher turret allowing the vehicle to fire from a position of cover.

While designs have evolved since the fall of the Soviet Union, the use of armoured forces to achieve a decisive result by a combination of mobility and firepower remains a standard tactic. Yet despite possessing a sufficient number and quality of tanks, Russian forces have relied more on infantry, with AFVs acting as fire-support platforms. Russia had some 3417 AFVs available at the start of the conflict, which suffered heavy losses to a variety of anti-tank weapons. This resulted in older vehicles being removed from storage and sent to the front. Ukraine's armoured forces were much smaller but were augmented by transfers of Western main battle tanks and other armoured vehicles. The performance of NATO AFVs in Ukrainian hands was watched with great interest worldwide.

A Russian Army T-80UE-1 tank is seen during the annual Army Games defence international technology exhibition.

T-54/T-55

The T-54 and T-55 are near-identical early post-war Soviet tanks. These World War II-era designs feature a bow machine gun on all but the last production models.

The Soviet T-34 was a formidable weapon but not without its problems. The transmission was notoriously prone to breakdowns, and the interior layout made operating the tank tiring and awkward for the crew. From 1944, the original 76.2mm (3in) gun was upgraded to a more effective 85mm (3.35in) weapon, with changes to the crew compartment resulting in a more crew-friendly vehicle. Naturally, even as the T-34 was maturing into its full potential a replacement was under development.

This project would result in the T-54, which entered production in 1947. It featured the low silhouette and rounded turret that would characterize Soviet tank designs over the next decade and mounted a 100mm (3.94in) rifled gun capable of penetrating any tank of the era. Continuous development resulted in a mature design designated T-55 in 1958. Most existing T-54s were modified to T-55 standard during their service life. An improved model,

designated T-55A, went into production in the 1960s. Vast numbers of T-54/T-55s were constructed, with production only ceasing in the early 1980s. As the conflict in Ukraine went on, Russia resorted to breaking T-55s out of storage in the hope of making good their losses.

New features

Early-production T-55s received a 12-cylinder diesel engine with 433kW (581bhp) and additional fuel, greatly increasing operational radius. The same 100mm (3.94in) main gun as was used on the T-54 was used on the T-55, though a bore gas extractor was added, and ammunition stowage increased from 30 to 45 rounds. Infrared sights and a stabilization system became standard on the T-55 and were retrofitted to earlier models. Improved ammunition provided armour penetration of 390mm (15.35in).

The T-55 also received an early NBC protection system. This was designed to

---

T-54/T-55

Weight: 36 tonnes (35.5 tons)
Length (with gun): 9.01m (29ft 6in)
Width: 3.15m (10ft 4in)
Height: 2.4m (7ft 11in)
Engine: V-55 V12-cylinder diesel, 388kW (520hp)
Maximum Road Speed: 55km/h (30mph)
Crew: 4
Armour Type: Min–Max Steel Rolled Homogenous Armour (RHA) 20–203mm (0.8–8in)
Main Armament: 100mm (3.94in) DT-10TG L/53.5 rifled cannon
Main Gun Ammunition Stowed: 34

T-55

From early 2023, the venerable T-55 was committed to replace losses among Russian armoured formations. Despite upgrades since its introduction this tank was unsuited to modern mobile armoured warfare. However, its gun could still provide direct-fire support in relatively static conditions. This artwork shows a T-55 fitted with an overhead cage, designed to deflect anti-armour missiles from above.

filter out particles, such as radioactive fallout, but would not protect against harmful gases. In the 1950s, there was a general belief that any future war would involve nuclear weapons, and the T-55 was tested to determine its survivability in the face of a tactical nuclear strike. The tank could withstand blast effects as close as 300m (984ft) from ground zero, though the crew would not survive the thermal pulse and radiation closer than 700m (2297ft).

Further upgrades

The T-55 continued to evolve during the 1970s and 1980s, gaining an improved engine and suspension, better gun stabilization and targeting,

IMPROVED ARMOUR

Other local expedients also emerged during the conflict, with Russian vehicles gaining additional protection in the form of logs or even lumps of rubble. More sophisticated efforts included slat armour improvised out of bars of metal and contraptions made from wire and fence components. These might be sufficient to detonate a shaped-charge away from the armour, but they are no substitute for proper explosive reactive armour.

smoke grenade launchers and a laser rangefinder for the main gun. Armour was also improved, including expedients such as skirts and screens to detonate an RPG or similar weapon short of the tank.

Despite these improvements, the T-55 remains a Cold War tank rooted in

World War II thinking. Any tank is better than no tanks, but these elderly vehicles are very vulnerable on the battlefield. As AFV design has improved, anti-tank weapons have been developed to tackle much better-protected targets. However, the T-55 is a relatively simple vehicle and is available in huge numbers.

T-62

The Soviet successor to the T-54/55, the T-62 offered better protection, a bigger gun and greatly improved crew spaces.

T-62

Weight: 41.8 tonnes (41.1 tons)
Length (with gun): 9.33m (30ft 6in)
Width: 3.3m (10ft 9in)
Height: 2.39m (7ft 9in)
Engine: V-55U diesel, 462kW (620hp)
Maximum Road Speed: 52km/h (32mph)
Crew: 4
Armour Type: 20–242mm (0.8–9.5in) RHA + composite appliqué + side skirts
Main Armament: 115mm (4.5in) U-5TS (2A20) L/49.5 smoothbore cannon
Main Gun Ammunition Stowed: 42

Development of a new medium tank began almost as soon as the T-55 was accepted for service, and the new tank was largely derived from it. The original specifications called for the T-62, as the new design came to be called, to be capable of withstanding the T-55's 100mm (3.94in) main gun. The prototype was ready in 1959, with the T-62 entering service in 1961. The T-62 design drew heavily on the T-55 and used some of the same components.

T-62M

The T-62 is a derivative of the T-55, most easily distinguished by the spacing of its road wheels. This example wears the 'Z' identification symbol used by Russian forces fighting in Ukraine.

The chief improvements were in the turret; despite being larger than that of the T-55, it weighs about the same and offers improved protection largely due to its shaping. The main gun of the T-62 was the first smoothbore weapon adopted by the Soviet armed forces.

Return to service

Although Russian production ceased in 1973, T-62s were licence-built elsewhere until the 1980s. Large numbers were put into storage as they were replaced by more modern vehicles, and after suffering huge tank losses in Ukraine, 800 of these were reactivated under a refurbishment programme to be completed in 2025.

The T-62 was well protected against the threats of its time but is vulnerable to many of today's anti-tank weapons. Nevertheless, it will be many years before Russia can bring its modern tank strength back up, so these upgraded T-62s will have to prop up Russian armoured forces for some time to come.

A damaged Russian T-62 tank sits abandoned by the roadside south of the village of Novovorontsovka, Kherson Oblast, southern Ukraine, October 2022.

T-64

Unlike the T-62, the T-64 was not exported. Large numbers were inherited by Russia and Ukraine following the breakup of the Soviet Union.

The T-64 was defined as a main battle tank rather than a medium tank (as the T-62 had been). The primary reason for this redesignation was the fully stabilized main gun, which was increased in calibre to 115mm (4.53in) and supported by an autoloader. Composite armour was used for the first time on a Soviet tank. Deliveries to the Red Army began in 1963, though the outside world did not become aware of the new design for some years.

Teething troubles

The autoloader was not without its problems but did allow a reduction in crew to three and a consequently smaller turret without undue cramping. The first production models were powered by a 522kw (700hp) diesel engine derived from the powerpack used in the British Chieftain. It was not a success and was replaced with improved but still rather unreliable 5TD and 5TDF engines. The main advantage was compactness, trading becoming a smaller target for increased maintenance burdens.

Improved versions of the T-64 continued to appear, including the T-64A, which featured a 125mm (4.92in) smoothbore gun that could penetrate the frontal armour of all contemporary Western main battle tanks. The T-64A also had upgraded protection and a remote-controlled machine gun on the turret top, and reliability issues were tackled. This variant was officially adopted for service in 1973.

The T-64B model added the capability to launch 9K112 Kobra anti-tank missiles through its main gun and was accompanied by a T64B1 version with the same general upgrades but no missile capability. Improvements in powerplant eventually led to the T-64B1M. Its 746kW (1000hp) 6TD diesel engine offered greater mobility and reliability over previous variants. The T-64BV added enhanced armour protection and the ability to use explosive reactive armour. T-64s built from 1983 to 1985 were to this standard, with older vehicles upgraded to it or towards it.

T-64

Weight: 39.3 tonnes (38.7 tons)
Length (with gun): 9.22m (30ft 3in)
Width: 3.41m (11ft 2in)
Height: 2.17m (7ft 2in)
Engine: 6TD diesel, 746kW (1000hp)
Maximum Road Speed: 60km/h (37mph)
Crew: 3
Armour Type: 20–355mm (0.8–14in) RHA + composite + side skirts
Main Armament: 125mm (4.92in) D-81TM (2A46M-1) L/48.6 smoothbore cannon
Main Gun Ammunition Stowed: 36

T-64BV

The T-64 and variants are deployed by both sides in the Ukraine-Russia conflict. This example wears Russian identification symbols. Its explosive reactive armour (ERA) is clearly evident along the hull flanks and front of the turret.

A platoon of Ukrainian T-64s undergo tank drills somewhere in the Kyiv region, February 2020.

Ukrainian variants

The T-64 was the main Ukrainian battle tank at the outbreak of the conflict. The T-64BM Bulat is an upgraded version featuring a 634kW (850hp) 5TDFM or 746kW (1000hp) 6TD-1 engine, improved fire control and add-on ERA. The T-64BM, also known as T-64U, entered service with Ukrainian armed forces in 2005.

An alternative variant, designated T-64BM2 and featuring an autoloader for the main gun, was not selected.

Other Ukrainian variants include the T-64E, which was aimed at the export market, and specialist vehicles, including the BREAM-64 armoured recovery vehicle and MT-64 armoured bridgelayer. Command tank versions of contemporary variants have also appeared over the years.

The T-64BM saw action from 2014 onwards against T-64s supplied by Russia to eastern Ukrainian separatists but was retired from front-line service before the Russian invasion. An upgraded version, designated T-64BM2, was ordered in 2021.

In the interim, the mainstay of Ukrainian armoured forces was the T-64BV, with a 125mm (4.92in) gun capable of launching anti-tank missiles. These vehicles proved effective, but heavy losses prompted appeals for Western AFVs to replace them.

T-64BM Bulat

This Ukrainian T-64BM Bulat has a modern look that belies its origins. With a more powerful engine and advanced fire control these tanks are closer to new designs than their Cold War ancestors.

T-72 & T90

The T-72 Ural was developed as a low-cost alternative to the T-64 and became the basis for a large family of upgraded versions and variants.

The prototype T-72 was produced in 1968, formally entering service in 1973. Of the 17,831 T-72s eventually produced, only 950 were to the original specification – to create a cheaper alternative to the T-64 that could withstand the 105mm (4.13in) guns standard at that time on NATO tanks, though only in the frontal arc and from a range of greater than 500m (1640ft). The T-72 mounted a 125mm (4.92in) gun fed by an autoloader, which, although slower than the T-64's autoloader, was more reliable.

Despite being a low-cost alternative, the T-72 incorporated some improvements over the T-64. Its suspension was better, and the roadwheel design reverted to the type used on the T-55 and T-62. The steel roadwheels used on the T-64 offered some advantages but made the vehicle hard to recover after a track loss, causing a return to the aluminium roadwheels used by earlier vehicles.

Compared to Western tanks of the time, the T-72 had a more potent gun but less effective fire control. Night vision was also rather poor, and a laser rangefinder was only added on upgraded versions. The tank could self-entrench with a retractable blade and could wade through water obstacles up to 5m (16.4ft) deep without additional assistance.

Upgrades and variants

The T-72 Ural-1 was accepted by the Soviet Army in 1975. It featured a thermal sleeve for the gun and an infrared searchlight on the gunner's side of the turret. Armour was improved, and from 1977 onwards, the turret received composite armour. An export version was also created to a lower specification.

Adopted in 1979, the T-72A gained additional armour and a laser rangefinder along with increased ammunition capacity and an improved gun with better sights. The 582kW (780hp) engine was upgraded twice, with post-1984 vehicles using a 626kW (840hp) diesel engine. As usual, an export version (designated T-72M) was made available. This

---

T-72AMT

Weight: 46.5 tonnes (45.7 tons)
Length (with gun): 9.54m (31ft 4in)
Width: 3.6m (11ft 8in)
Height: 2.23m (7ft 4in)
Engine: V-46-6 V12-cylinder diesel engine, 582kW (780hp)
Maximum Road Speed: 60km/h (37mph)
Crew: 3
Armour Type: 380mm (15in) Steel RHA
Main Armament: 125mm (4.92in) 2A46M2 L/48 smoothbore cannon
Main Gun Ammunition Stowed: 44

T-72AMT

The T-72 can be considered the definitive Russian main battle tank. Its low silhouette is well suited to the rapid mobile combat envisaged at the time of its design.

was then upgraded and redesignated T-72M1.

The T-72B gained explosive reactive armour as well as improved turret protection. It became the standard production model from the mid-1980s and saw action in the invasion of Ukraine. The T-72S export version has less protection against NBC weapons but is otherwise similar. Another improved T-72A, designated T-72AV, was an upgrade package mainly focused on armour protection.

The last mass-production version of the T-72 was designated T-72BM, with better reactive armour. It entered production in 1988 but was replaced by the T-90. Developed from the T-72 during the period of financial troubles following the collapse of the Soviet Union, the T-90 essentially mated the T-80's turret to a T-72 chassis and was

highly successful on the international market. Since this period, Russia has tended to mass-produce upgraded T-72 models or upgrade older tanks, with no large-scale production of new designs.

The T-72 became the mainstay of Soviet armoured forces and was widely exported, with licence-built versions in India and Eastern Europe. Different variants are likely to be encountered in Ukraine as older tanks are brought back into service, with or without upgrade packages.

Polish T-72 derivatives

The Polish PT-91 Twardy ('Hard') is derived from the T-72 but is significantly more capable than the T-72s in Russian hands. The Twardy was developed from the T-72A. However, whilst it retains the same overall appearance, it has

Massed tank parades have been a regular feature of Red Square military displays for many years, with the T-72 symbolizing Russian military might in terms of both numbers and reputation. That reputation was severely undermined in Ukraine.

an upgraded 634kW (850hp) engine and improved transmission. The same 125mm (4.92in) gun is used, with an improved autoloader and better stabilization.

The gun is supported by advanced electronic systems not apparent at first glance. However, such systems make the PT-91 a modern tank rather than a late Cold War design. Poland originally offered 60 PT-91s – a very significant force, considering the losses taken by both sides – with the possibility of more in the future. Poland also offered support and repairs for other tanks, such as the Leopard 2.

T-72B

The T-72B was an upgraded version introduced in 1985, and included a 9K120 Svir guided missile system and thicker, spaced composite turret armour.

T-72B

Weight: 41.5 tonnes (40.8 tons)
Length (with gun): 9.24m (30ft 3in)
Width: 3.6m (11ft 8in)
Height: 2.37m (7ft 8in)
Engine: V-55 V12-cylinder diesel engine, 582kW (780hp)
Maximum Road Speed: 42km/h (26mph)
Crew: 3
Armour Type: Steel RHA + Spaced + Composite + ERA + Side-skirts
Main Armament: 125mm (4.92in) 2A46M2 L/48 smoothbore cannon
Main Gun Ammunition Stowed: 38

T-90

Weight: 41.5 tonnes (40.8 tons)
Length (with gun): 9.24m (30ft 3in)
Width: 3.6m (11ft 8in)
Height: 2.37m (7ft 8in)
Engine: V-55 V12-cylinder diesel engine, 582kW (780hp)
Maximum Road Speed: 42km/h (26mph)
Crew: 3
Armour Type: Steel RHA + Spaced + Composite + ERA + Side-skirts
Main Armament: 125mm (4.92in) 2A46M2 L/48 smoothbore cannon
Main Gun Ammunition Stowed: 38

T-90

The T-90 is a development of the T-72, incorporating weapon systems from the T-80. It went into production in 1994, with 750–1000 eventually built. No new Russian MBTs have been developed since the T-90; instead the focus has been on upgrading existing designs. The T-90 incorporates the Shtora-1 electro-optical countermeasures system, which can defeat some infrared and laser guidance systems. However, it is not effective against the most recent anti-tank weapons such as Javelin. Reportedly, less than 200 T-90s were operational at the beginning of the conflict in Ukraine, and those committed were soon withdrawn after taking unacceptable losses.

T-90K

Although it was the most modern main battle tank used by Russia during the invasion of Ukraine, the T-90 took unacceptable losses during the first year and were withdrawn – though not before some examples were captured and turned against their former owners.

T-80

The T-80 was developed from the highly successful T-64 main battle tank. Various versions took part in the Russia-Ukraine conflict.

T-80BVM

At the time of the Russian invasion, Ukraine possessed 271 T-80 main battle tanks. Russia considered removing theirs from service due to the difficulty of maintaining them compared to T-72 derivatives.

Whereas the T-72 was developed as a cheaper alternative to the T-64, the T-80 was to be its successor as the most capable Soviet main battle tank. In addition to improving off-road performance and eliminating some of the problems of the T-64, the T-80 was given a 746kW (1000hp) gas turbine engine. Gas turbines have the advantage of compactness but require more maintenance than diesel ones. The former were notoriously fuel-hungry at the time the T-80 was put into production. As a result, the majority of T-80s produced were held in reserve, with cheaper diesel-powered T72s taking centre stage.

Developed versions

All versions of the T-80 use a 125mm (4.92in) smoothbore gun fed by an autoloader. The 1978 T-80B model gained the ability to launch anti-tank missiles through its gun and was upgraded to T-80BV standard with explosive reactive armour. This variant was available in large numbers for the invasion of Ukraine, though it suffered heavily from anti-tank weapons. The T-80U is a further upgraded model with a more powerful gas turbine engine –

originally 820kW (1100hp), and then 932kW (1250hp) on later models. Meanwhile, a diesel-powered T-80UD variant was intended to become the Soviet main battle tank of choice. The collapse of the Soviet Union derailed this plan, leaving examples in both Russian and Ukrainian hands. Development has continued, culminating in the Russian-made T-80BVM, which has thermal sights and better armour protection.

T-80BVM

Weight: 44.5 tonnes (43.8 tons)
Length (with gun): 9.9m (32ft 5in)
Width: 3.4m (11ft 1in)
Height: 2.2m (7ft 2in)
Engine: GTD-1250 gas turbine, 932kW (1250hp)
Maximum Road Speed: 68km/h (42mph)
Crew: 3
Armour Steel RHA + Composite + ERA + Side-skirts
Main Armament: 125mm (4.92in) 2A46M L/48 smoothbore cannon
Main Gun Ammunition Stowed: 40

Ukrainian T-80UD tanks undergo training near Zhytomir in 2018.

T-14 Armata

Although presented to the world as a game-changing weapon system, the T-14 Armata has not made any impact on the Ukraine conflict.

The T-14 Armata represents a new generation of highly automated combat vehicles. The crew are all located in an armoured fighting compartment in the front of the hull, increasing personnel survivability even if the turret is disabled.

At the rear of the hull is the power compartment, housing an engine that has reportedly been the source of problems throughout the development process. Russian secrecy has clouded the issue, but it appears that the original powerpack was unsatisfactory and the obvious replacements would not fit on the T-14's engine bay.

Unmanned turret

The T-14 Armata's turret is unmanned, mounting a 125mm (4.92in) main gun that may eventually be upgraded to a 152mm (5.98in) weapon. It can launch guided missiles and is supported by a remote-controlled mount that can reportedly carry a machine gun or a large-calibre grenade launcher. The vehicle's protection reflects modern realities – the front has explosive reactive armour to enhance its passive armour protection, while the flanks and

T-14 Armata

The T-14 Armata has been dogged by delays and difficulties. Around 2300 were originally ordered, for delivery by 2020. Only a fraction of that number was available in 2023, and Russian forces reportedly did not want to deploy them to combat zones due to their continuing unreliability.

rear are covered by slat armour to detonate rocket-propelled grenades and similar projectiles short of the intended target.

Late deployment

It might have been expected that the T-14 would lead the invasion of Ukraine. Reportedly, nearly 200 were available at the outbreak of the conflict. However, the early assaults were led by older models, in particular the T-72 and T-90.

Rumours in 2022 indicated imminent deployment, and the RIA state news agency reported in April 2023 that T-14 Armatas had been used to fire on Ukrainian positions, but had not been used in any direct assaults, mainly, it is thought, because of their lack of combat readiness.

T-14 Armata
Weight: 48 tonnes (47.2 tons)
Length (with gun): 10.3m (33ft 9in)
Width: 3.5m (11ft 6in)
Height: 3.3m (10ft 8in)
Engine: ChTZ 12N360 A-85-3A X-12 diesel, 1119kW (1500hp)
Maximum Road Speed: 80km/h (50mph)
Crew: 3
Armour Type: RHA + composite + Dual-ERA + APS + side-skirts
Main Armament: 125mm (4.92in) 2A82-1M L/55 smoothbore cannon
Main Gun Ammunition Stowed: 45

Leopard 2

The Leopard 2 has its origins in the US-German MBT-70 programme, which became mired in cost and technical problems.

After withdrawing from MBT-70, Germany was able to make use of some of the technologies and concepts developed in the project, creating a tank that had much in common with the US M1 Abrams but also retained a distinctly European character. Leopard 2 was adopted for German service in 1979 and has achieved considerable export success. Using composite armour similar to British Chobham armour, the Leopard 2 mounts a stabilized 120mm (4.72in) smoothbore gun capable of penetrating the frontal armour of a T-72 at 2000m (6562ft) with the correct ammunition. Hulls are no longer in production, but existing tanks are upgraded to newer specifications as they become available. The design has gone through several upgrade programmes, with different users possessing various models.

Leopard 2A4

The Leopard 2A4 is the main version deployed. Several nations offered Leopards to Ukraine, making it numerically the most important foreign AFV in the conflict.

Ukrainian deployment

The Leopard 2 may be the most important Western AFV to be supplied to Ukraine. This is largely due to its numbers and the availability of support in nearby countries. Success in combat inevitably comes at the cost of destroyed and disabled vehicles. However, the Leopard 2 is designed to be far more survivable than equivalent Russian tanks. Its ammunition is stored in such a way that an explosion blows out panels on the turret bustle rather than being directed inwards, making a Leopard 2 more likely to be repairable.

Support from countries such as Poland ensured that most disabled Leopards were able to return to service. Ukraine deployed at least 70 Leopard 2 tanks as part of its summer 2023 offensive, with reports of a small number being damaged or destroyed.

Leopard 1A5

At least 100 older Leopard 1A5 tanks have also been donated to the Ukrainian armed forces by Denmark, Germany and the Netherlands. Some of this batch were delivered in the summer of 2023, and an additional 100 were planned for early 2024. These obsolete tanks require more time to upgrade and prepare for active deployment, and have yet to see combat in Ukraine.

Leopard 2A4

Weight: 56 tonnes (55.1 tons)
Length (with gun): 9.66m (31ft 1in)
Width: 3.7m (12ft 1in)
Height: 3m (9 ft 11in)
Engine: MTU MB 873 12-cylinder multi-fuel diesel, 1119 kW (1500hp)
Maximum Road Speed: 70km/h (43mph)
Crew: 4
Armour Composite + Side-Skirts
Main Armament: Rheinmetall 120mm (4.72in) L/44 smoothbore cannon
Main Gun Ammunition Stowed: 42

Challenger 2

The British-made Challenger 2 main battle tank entered service in 1998. Small numbers were supplied to the Ukrainian armed forces along with the training to operate them.

Challenger 2

The Challenger 2 was developed with a defensive style of warfare in mind, stemming massed Soviet armoured assaults from a hull-down position.

Challenger 2

At the time of writing, the 82nd Air Assault Brigade is the sole Ukrainian user of British-supplied Challenger 2 MBTs. At least one has been lost in action.

The flat planes of tanks such as the Challenger result from the use of ceramic/metal composite armour, which is difficult to cast in curved shapes. Composite armour is more resilient than simple steel, and sloping the armour increases the depth of penetration needed to reach the tank's interior. Additional protection is provided by smoke grenade dischargers and the ability to generate smoke by injecting oil into the hot exhausts. Most Russian tanks have had this capability since World War II.

The main gun normally uses High-explosive Squad Head (HESH) or Armour-Piercing Fin-stabilized Discarding Sabot (APFSDS) ammunition. Smoke rounds are also available as are Depleted Uranium (DU) penetrator rounds. Whether to supply DU ammunition to Ukraine or not was a controversial decision. However, both the USA and the UK eventually agreed to do so. The gun is fully stabilized and supported by advanced night vision and targeting systems tied into a battlefield information system that may permit advanced tanks such as the Challenger and the M1 Abrams to act as force multipliers for older and less well-equipped vehicles.

In the UK, Ukrainian crews completed training in March 2023. The impact a small force of 14 tanks might have on a major conflict is at the time

Challenger 2

Weight: 63.5 tonnes (62 tons)
Length (with gun): 13.5m (44ft 6in)
Width: 3.5m (11ft 6in)
Height: 2.5m (8ft 2in)
Engine: Perkins Condor CV12 TCA 26l diesel, 895kW (1200hp)
Maximum Road Speed: 59km/h (37mph)
Crew: 4
Armour Composite + ERA + Slat + Side-skirts
Main Armament: 120mm (4.7in) ROF L30A1 L/55 rifled cannon
Main Gun Ammunition Stowed: 52

of writing an open question, but Ukraine has demonstrated the ability to use advanced weapon systems in creative ways to achieve results before.

Abrams M1

The Abrams M1 has been in service since 1980 and has been repeatedly upgraded. The USA sent enough to Ukraine to outfit a complete battalion.

Development of the Abrams M1 began in the ill-fated US-German MBT-70 programme. After Germany pulled out in favour of developing what would become the Leopard 2 main battle tank, the US switched to a goal of cost-effectiveness rather than maximized capability at any cost. The prototypes used a 105mm (4.13in) gun, but this was increased to 120mm (4.72in) in later models. This was housed in a turret designed to carry modern sighting equipment such as laser rangefinders rather than retrofitting these as was necessary on older designs.

A US Army M1A1 Abrams tank needed for training Ukrainian tanks crews awaits offloading at Grafenwoehr, Germany, May 2023.

High-maintenance machines

The Abrams' gas turbine engine is relatively quiet compared to a diesel but became notorious for its high fuel consumption. Its 1119kW (1500hp) output provides very high open-ground speed and excellent cross-country performance. Developed versions improved fuel economy, but the Abrams still requires a high level of maintenance to keep it combat-worthy. As a result, providing a force of M1s to Ukraine was not a simple matter. The M1A2 version

was originally intended to be the version supplied, but it was quicker to send refurbished and upgraded M1A1s as they were already available.

The Abrams has already seen action against Russian tank designs, such as the T-72, during operations against Iraqi armoured forces. Several M1s received direct hits from the main armament of T72s without sustaining significant damage. The Abrams appears to be nearly invulnerable to the weapons carried by these vehicles.

Abrams M1A1

Weight: 61 tonnes (60 tons)
Length (with gun): 9.75m (32ft)
Width: 3.65m (11ft 11in)
Height: 2.88m (9ft 5in)
Engine: Lycoming/Honeywell AGT 1500 multi-fuel gas turbine, 1119kW (1500hp)
Maximum Road Speed: 72km/h (45mph)
Crew: 4
Armour Composite + Side-skirts
Main Armament: 105mm (4.1in) M60A1 L/55 rifled gun
Main Gun Ammunition Stowed: 55

Abrams M1A1

The US-built M1 Abrams MBT has faced its likely opponents – notably T-72 variants – before, and has dominated them.

BMP series

The BMP-1 was the world's first infantry fighting vehicle (IFV), not only carrying infantry to combat in relative safety but also capable of supporting them and successfully engaging some enemy armoured vehicles.

Adopted by the Soviet Army in 1966, the BMP-1 is armoured against 12.7mm (0.5in) machine gun fire in the forward arc and small arms elsewhere. It is armed with a 73mm (2.87in) smoothbore gun with a coaxial machine gun, offering some fire support capability against personnel and lightly armoured targets. A wire-guided 9K11 Malyutka missile mounted above the gun offers some anti-tank capability.

The vehicle is powered by a 224kW (300hp) diesel engine and is amphibious, propelling itself in water by rotation of the tracks. Personnel can fight from inside the vehicle using firing ports, though experience has shown that fire on the move is extremely inaccurate. Infantry enter and leave the vehicle through rear doors which contain fuel tanks, potentially causing a disaster if they are set alight.

BMP-2

Developed from the BMP-1, the BMP-2 entered service in the late 1970s and was produced in large numbers

in Russia as well as under licence elsewhere. It is visually similar to the BMP-1 but mounts a two-man turret containing a 30mm (1.18in) cannon. This is more likely to achieve hits than the unstabilized 73mm (2.87in) gun of the BMP-1 and is a more effective weapon overall. Like the BMP-1, the BMP-2 can launch a guided missile – either a 9K111 Fagot or 9K113 Konkurs – for anti-tank work. Many vehicles carry a ground launcher for the same missile.

The BMP-2 uses an improved version of the same engine as its predecessor and can carry seven troops rather than the 10–11 on board the BMP-1. Protection is not very different from the BMP-1; its armour will resist heavy machine gun fire from the front and small arms or shell fragments elsewhere. There is no mine protection, but the BMP-2 does have an NBC protection system and automated fire suppression.

The BMP-2M variant has upgraded electronics and sighting, supporting a

BMP-1AM

Weight: 13.7 tonnes (13.5 tons)
Length (with gun): 6.74m (22ft 1in)
Width: 2.94 (9ft 7in)
Height: 2.15m (7ft 1in)
Engine: UTD-20/3 diesel, 224kW (300hp)
Maximum Road Speed: 65km/h (40mph)
Crew: 3 (+ 7–8 troops)
Armour Type: 6–33mm (0.2–1.3in) RHA
Main Armament: 30mm (0.6in) 2A72 autocannon
Main Gun Ammunition Stowed: 760

30mm (1.18in) cannon, 30mm (1.18in) grenade launcher and four launchers for 9M133 Kornet anti-tank missiles. The manual transmission of the BMP-2 has been replaced with an automatic system, and the engine is variously rated as 268kW (360hp) or 298kW (400hp).

BMP-3

The BMP-3 carries seven infantry personnel like its predecessor, but has a more powerful 373kW (500hp) engine and better electronics. Its primary armament is a 100mm (3.94in) gun/missile launcher fed by

an autoloader. Its effective range against infantry and lightly armoured targets is given as 4000m (13,123ft). In addition, it can launch the 9K116 Bastion laser-guided missile, which is effective against armoured vehicles and low-flying helicopters. Many variants of these vehicles have been produced, along with upgrades and conversions. They may be encountered in many roles including light armoured reconnaissance, but even though the BMP-3 could be mistaken visually for a light tank it is vulnerable to almost any anti-armour weapon.

BMP-2

A BMP-2 in Russian markings. Some estimates suggest that Russia has more than 2000 BMP-2s deployed in Ukraine.

BMP-3

Weight: 18.9 tonnes (18.5 tons)
Length (with gun): 7.14m (23ft 5in)
Width: 3.3 (10ft 11in)
Height: 2.5m (8ft 2in)
Engine: UTD-32 diesel, 373kW (500hp)
Maximum Road Speed: 72km/h (45mph)
Crew: 3 (+ 7 troops)
Armour Type: Aluminium alloy/RHA + ERA + APS
Main Armament: 100mm (3.9in) 2A70 rifled autocannon
Main Gun Ammunition Stowed: 40

BMP-3

The BMP-3 features detection and tracking radar and an automated system to select ammunition and conduct defensive fire. This is augmented by the Shtora defensive system which can defeat some guided anti-tank weapons.

BMD series

The BMD series of armoured vehicles was developed to provide armoured transport and support to Russian airborne forces.

BMD-2

The BMD-2 was given a 30mmm cannon in place of the inaccurate 76mm gun used by its predecessor, mounted on a high-elevation turret to allow engagement of targets in high positions. This was implemented due to experiences in Afghanistan but may prove useful in urban combat.

The BMD-1 entered service in 1969. It mounted the same turret as the BMP-1 but carried only four troops in addition to its crew of three. Its lightweight armour provided protection from small-arms fire but could be penetrated by heavy machine guns. Although manufactured in smaller numbers than the BMP series, production was still significant, and examples of all models may be encountered in the Ukraine conflict.

Entering service in 1985, the BMD-2 is armed with a 30mm (1.18in) autocannon and an anti-tank missile. Unlike the BMD-1, it was not possible to simply use the turret from the equivalent BMP vehicle. A smaller one-man version was developed instead. Still very lightly protected and capable

of carrying only four infantry, the BMD-2 is highly mobile and altogether more effective than the BMD-1.

In 1990, the BMD-3 entered service. Plans to arm it with a 100mm (3.94in) gun produced a vehicle that took up too much space in a transport aircraft. A 30mm (1.18in) cannon was fitted instead but in a two-man turret.

The most recent iteration is BMD-4, which is larger and can carry six personnel in addition to its two-man crew. This version mounts a 100mm (3.94in) gun and a 30mm (1.18in)

autocannon backed up by anti-tank missiles. Its 373kW (500hp) engine provides very good offroad mobility. The BMD-4 entered Russian service in 2016.

BMD-2

Weight: 11.5 tonnes (11.3 tons)
Length (with gun): 7.85m (25ft 9in)
Width: 3.13m (10ft 3in)
Height: 2.45m (8ft 1in)
Engine: 5D-20 diesel, 331kW (450hp)
Maximum Road Speed: 80km/h (50mph)
Crew: 4 (+ 4 troops)
Armour Type: 10–15mm (0.4–0.6in) RHA
Main Armament: 30mm (1.2in) 2A42 autocannon
Main Gun Ammunition Stowed: 300

BMD-4

The BMD-4 carries a 100mm gun, which was the intended armament of the BMD-2.

BDRM series

The BDRM series began in 1959 with the BDRM-1, a turretless four-wheel-drive scout car. It became the standard Warsaw Pact light armoured reconnaissance vehicle.

Although humble compared to main battle tanks, armoured reconnaissance vehicles play a vital role in modern warfare. In addition to their obvious scouting capability, they are well suited to patrolling supply routes and providing rear-area security. The original BDRM-1 was a rather basic vehicle, though it featured a tyre pressure regulation system to improve offroad performance. It was also amphibious, using a water jet to propel itself. The original model was followed by variants specializing in NBC reconnaissance and command functions and a missile-armed light tank destroyer.

BDRM-2

The BDRM-2 entered service in 1962 and remains in service. It is better protected than the original vehicle, though only against splinters and small-arms fire. A one-man turret carrying a heavy machine gun was added, while the hull can carry additional personnel or be configured as necessary for specialist roles. The BDRM family has been the subject of upgrade programmes in recent years and is likely to remain in service for some time to come.

Missile carrier

The 9P148 is based on the BDRM-2. It is armed with five 9M113 Konkurs missile launchers on a retractable launch platform, with a total of 10 reloads carried within the vehicle. This vehicle was widely exported and remains in service with the Russian army, providing mobile and inexpensive anti-tank capability.

BDRM/9P148

Mounting man-portable anti-armour missiles on a light armoured chassis creates a highly mobile platform that can function as a tank destroyer in the right conditions. The short range and limited effectiveness of the missiles makes this a high-risk mission.

BDRM/9P148

Weight: 7 tonnes (6.9 tons)
Length 5.75m (18ft 10in)
Width: 2.35m (7ft 8in)
Height: 2.01m (6ft 7in)
Engine: GAZ-140 V-8 petrol, 104kW (140hp)
Maximum Road Speed: 100km/h (62mph)
Crew: 2–3
Armour Type: Steel RHA
Main Armament: 9M113 Konkurs (AT-5 'Spandrel') ATGM
Main Gun Ammunition Stowed: 15

BTR-60 & BTR-70

The BTR-60 is an eight-wheel-drive armoured personnel carrier (APC) dating from the early Cold War period.

Armoured vehicle design is always a trade-off between assets. Wheeled vehicles are cheaper to construct and easier to maintain than their tracked equivalents, though they generally have inferior off-road performance. On the other hand, strategic mobility is better as wheeled vehicles can travel faster under their own power and do less damage to the roads they pass over.

Open-top original

The BTR-60 was developed from 1957–60 and was in production until 1976. The original model had an open top, leaving the 14 infantry personnel it carried highly vulnerable to shell fragments. Developed versions gained a solid roof and NBC protection along with a small turret mounting a heavy machine gun.

Many variants

The basic BTR-60 was very lightly protected but suitable for conversion to other roles. Variants included

BTR-60

Where the BTR-60 has been called out of reserve to replace losses of more advanced vehicles, it joins a general downward trend in capability while enabling Russian forces to keep up the fight.

command, communication and artillery observation vehicles along with various experimental modifications. The BTR-60Z gained a new turret which was used on the BTR-70. Over 25,000 BTR-60s were built by the former Soviet Union, with others produced under licence elsewhere.

Storage

Almost all the remaining BTR-60s in the Russian inventory were in storage at the outbreak of conflict in Ukraine, as were most of the BTR-70s still in service. Losses of other vehicles may require large numbers of these elderly and rather vulnerable transports to be pulled out of reserve and sent to join the fighting.

BTR-60

Weight: 10.3 tonnes (10.1 tons)
Length 7.56m (24ft 9in)
Width: 2.83 (9ft 3in)
Height: 2.31m (7ft 7in)
Engine: Two GAZ-40P petrol, each 67kW (90hp)
Maximum Road Speed: 80km/h (50mph)
Crew: 2 (+ 14 troops)
Armour Type: 5–9mm (0.2–0.4in) steel RHA
Main Armament: 14.5mm (0.6in) PVKT heavy machine gun
Main Gun Ammunition Stowed: 2100

BTR-70

The fully amphibious BTR-70 is armed with one heavy and one light machine guns mounted in its small turret. Examples have served with both Ukraine and Russia (shown here).

BTR-70

Weight: 11.5 tonnes (11.3 tons)

Length 7.5m (24ft 7in)

Width: 2.80 (9ft 2in)

Height: 2.31m (7ft 7in)

Engine: twin GAZ-495 petrol engines, 86kW (115hp)

Maximum Road Speed: 80km/h (50mph)

Crew: 3 (+ 7 troops)

Armour Type: 7–9mm (0.3–0.4in) steel RHA

Main Armament: 14.5mm (0.6in) KPVT heavy machine gun; coaxial 7.62mm (0.3in) PKT MG

Main Gun Ammunition Stowed: 500

Ukrainian infantry evacuate a BTR-80 during a training exercise in 2015. The photograph shows the soldiers armed with AK-74 assault rifles.

BTR-80 & BTR-82

Lessons learned with the BTR-60 and BTR-70 were incorporated into a new generation of highly mobile light armoured personnel carriers.

The basic concept of the eight-wheel-drive APC was well-proven when work began on the BTR-80. Lessons learned in Afghanistan prompted a move from twin petrol engines to a single diesel, reducing the chance of fire and explosion. The turret of the BTR-70, mounting a 14.5mm (0.57in) machine gun, was used with some modifications. Notably, this included a higher maximum elevation made necessary by ambushes as Russian convoys moved through the steep-sided valleys of Afghanistan.

Low silhouette

The resulting vehicle is visually very similar to the BTR-60 it was intended to replace, with the same low silhouette and compact turret. It is armoured only against small-arms fire, though there is an NBC protection system. It can carry seven infantrymen in addition to its crew of three. Firing ports along the sides allow infantry to use their weapons from behind armour, though effectiveness from a moving vehicle is questionable.

BTR-82

Russia inherited around 3800 BTR-80s at the breakup of the Soviet Union and built more until 2004. These were the improved BTR-80S variant, with older vehicles upgraded to the same standard. From 2010, a further developed vehicle, designated BTR-82, was in production.

Incorporating composite armour and mine protection, the BTR-82 is more survivable than its predecessor. It mounts a 30mm (1.18in) cannon in a remote-controlled weapon station instead of the conical turret of earlier vehicles.

BTR-82

More recent armoured vehicles, such as the BTR-82, recognized the need for mine protection and incorporated better all-round survivability. The characteristic turret of the BTR-70 was replaced by a remote-controlled 30mm cannon mounting.

BTR-82

Weight: 15.4 tonnes (15.2 tons)
Length (with gun): 7.65m (25ft 1in)
Width: 2.9 (9ft 6in)
Height: 2.8m (9ft 2in)
Engine: KamAZ 740.14-300 diesel, 224kW (300hp)
Maximum Road Speed: 100km/h (62mph)
Crew: 3 (+ 7 troops)
Armour Type: RHA + composite
Main Armament: 30mm (1.2in) 2A72 dual-feed automatic cannon
Main Gun Ammunition Stowed: 400

BMTP 'Terminator'

The BMTP was developed as a result of Russian experiences in Afghanistan and Chechnya. It is intended to protect and support tanks operating in difficult terrain.

The Soviet-Afghan war was characterized by operations against enemy personnel high up on the sides of steep valleys – conditions not dissimilar to those encountered in urban terrain. The armoured vehicles available at the time could not engage targets high above them other than with machine guns mounted atop the hull or turret. This created conditions where otherwise potent vehicles were highly vulnerable.

T-72 chassis
The BMTP-1 was built on a T-72 chassis, mounting its weapons in a remote-controlled turret capable of high elevation. Various weapon fits are possible, including 30mm (1.18in) cannon, automatic grenade launchers and anti-tank missiles.

The BMPT-2 is virtually identical but is intended for the export market, fitted out as the client prefers. A new variant,

BMTP 'Terminator'

Tanks are notoriously vulnerable in close terrain. One Russian solution was to create 'tank escort' vehicles armed with anti-personnel weapons, providing defence against infantry without undermining the AFV's primary role.

designated BMTP-3, is based on the AT-14 Armata chassis.

Tank escort
The BMTP is intended to escort tanks in difficult terrain, engaging infantry positioned in high places such as the upper storeys of buildings or breaking up swarms of hostiles trying to assault the tank. Doctrine calls for two Terminators to protect each tank in urban terrain, and one Terminator to escort two tanks in more open areas. However, only very small numbers are available, so actual use will probably diverge from this intent.

BMTP 'Terminator'
Weight: 48.9 tonnes (48.1 tons)
Length: 7.2m (23ft 7in)
Width: 3.8m (12ft 6in)
Height: 3.37m (11ft 1in)
Engine: V-92S2 V12-cylinder diesel, 736kW (1000hp)
Maximum Road Speed: 60km/h (37mph)
Crew: 5
Armour Type: RHA + modular composite + ERA + partially slatted side skirts
Main Armament: 30mm (1.18in) 2A42 autocannon
Main Gun Ammunition Stowed 850

KamAZ Typhoon-K protected truck

Logistics and utility vehicles are unglamorous, but no modern army could function without them. Recent experience has highlighted just how vulnerable these vehicles can be.

The KamAZ family includes four, six and eight-wheel vehicles, of which the six-wheel variant is most common. Internally, it consists of a driving compartment and a rear compartment, which can carry 14 personnel or be configured to suit a variety of requirements. Both compartments are lightly protected with steel/ceramic composite armour that will defeat small-arms fire and shell splinters. The underside of the vehicle is protected against mine and other explosive detonations, and an NBC protection system is standard.

Self-defence

The KamAZ is not routinely armed, though there are firing ports in the sides of the rear compartment. If necessary, a remote weapon station can be fitted atop the crew compartment, carrying a 7.62mm (0.3in) or 14.5mm (0.57in) machine gun. All-round observation using a five-camera system permits the crew to engage targets in any direction.

Whatever firepower may be available, survival in an ambush situation depends largely upon retaining the ability to move. All of the bullet-resistant tyres are run-flat, enabling the vehicle to drag itself out of trouble even if they are punctured. The need for such measures was demonstrated in conflicts from Iraq to Chechnya, and with Russian supply routes passing through occupied territory the likelihood of direct attack or encountering roadside bombs and mines is high.

KamAZ Typhoon-K

Protecting the supply lines is necessary, but places an additional burden on the fighting forces. Improved survivability for transport vehicles may be a cost-effective solution.

KamAZ 'Typhoon-K'
Weight: 21 tonnes (20.7 tons)
Length 8.99m (29ft 9in)
Width: 2.45m (8ft)
Height: 3.32m (10ft 9in)
Engine: KamAZ 740.354-450 diesel, 336kW (450hp)
Maximum Road Speed: 105km/h (65mph)
Crew: 2 (+ 16 troops)
Armour Type: RHA + composite
Main Armament: 14.5mm (0.57in) KPVT heavy machine gun or 7.62mm (0.3in) PKT machine gun
Main Gun Ammunition Stowed 500/1000

Varta APC

The Varta APC is a light personnel carrier and utility vehicle in service with Ukrainian forces. It can carry up to eight personnel in addition to its two-man crew.

The Varta APC was designed from the outset as a cost-effective transport vehicle reflecting the realities of the modern battlespace. It is armoured against small-arms fire and designed to survive mine attacks.

The V-shaped underside of the hull is intended to deflect blasts while passenger and crew seats are designed to protect the occupant from a blast originating beneath the vehicle. Fire suppression and air filtration systems are also fitted.

Mobility and flexibility

The vehicle is not armed as standard, though there are 10 firing ports for use by passengers. A roof mount can support a 7.62mm (0.3in) or 12.7mm (0.5in) machine gun, and a small turret can be fitted capable of mounting up to a 14.5mm (0.57in) machine gun.

The 224kW (300hp) six-cylinder diesel engine is designed to run on a variety of fuels, though performance

Varta APC

Modern armed forces have increasingly perceived a need for light vehicles capable of handling relatively minor threats such as insurgents with small arms. Mines and improvised explosive devices are a serious hazard in the environment where the Varta was expected to operate.

and maintenance requirements can be affected. The four-wheel-drive system uses an eight-speed transmission.

Although designated an armoured personnel carrier, the Varta is lightly protected as modern vehicles go. It is, however, well suited to a variety of roles, most of which do not require heavy protection.

As a relatively light vehicle, it has good strategic mobility on roads and can handle rough terrain. It is possible that these vehicles will be pressed into other roles, perhaps acting as carriers for shoulder-launched anti-tank and anti-aircraft missiles.

Varta APC
Weight: 17.5 tonnes (17.22 tons)
Length 6.8m (22.3ft)
Width: 2.55m (7.4ft)
Height: 4m (13.1ft)
Engine: six-cylinder, V6 turbocharged diesel engine, 223.8kW (300hp) and a maximum torque of 1128Nm
Maximum Road Speed: 100km/h (62mph)
Armour Type: STANAG 4569 level two protection
Crew: 2 + 8 personnel
Main Armament: Gunner's station on the roof, with 7.62mm (0.3in) PK machine gun

Novator APC

The Novator APC is a small utility vehicle developed in Ukraine. It can be configured as a personnel carrier, reconnaissance vehicle or light transport.

Although designated an armoured personnel carrier, the Novator is only protected against small-arms fire and relatively minor explosions such as grenades and undetonated artillery submunitions. In its carrier configuration, it can transport eight to 10 personnel. This figure is reduced to five in its reconnaissance configuration.

Combat module

The Novator APC can be fitted with an Iva combat module, which mounts a 12.7mm (0.5in) machine gun. Ukraine has built or ordered a variety of combat modules, some of which are suitable for small wheeled vehicles and some for larger armoured platforms. Self-contained mountings can be configured to the user's specification, typically mounting machine guns, light autocannon or infantry anti-tank weapons such as Javelin.

The addition of modern combat modules to older vehicles can provide the advantages of advanced imaging and targeting systems at a relatively low cost compared to a new-built vehicle. Such upgrades can be very successful but there is a limit to what can be achieved in the long run. Older vehicles may have maintenance or spares-procurement issues, or not be very well protected against weapons that emerged since they were designed.

Similarly, fitting weapons such as 30mm (1.18in) cannon and Javelin missiles to a light vehicle like Novator can create a vehicle whose ability to absorb damage does not match its capabilities – the proverbial eggshell armed with a hammer.

Novator APC

The Novator is another light transport and utility vehicle better suited to security work than warfare. The addition of self-contained weapon mounts can give it impressive firepower but ultimately it is still a lightly protected patrol vehicle.

Novator APC
Weight: 8.84 tonnes (8.7 tons)
Length 6.4m (21ft)
Width: 2.35m (7.7ft)
Height: 2.38m (7.8ft)
Engine: Ford V8 Super turbo diesel engine, 223.8kW (300hp) and a maximum torque of 996Nm
Maximum Road Speed: 140km/h (87mph)
Armour Type: Multi-layer bulletproof glass
Crew: 2 + 8 personnel
Main Armament: N/A

M113

The venerable M113 armoured personnel carrier is a versatile vehicle, but it is vulnerable to many threats on today's battlefield.

The M113 entered service in 1960 and has seen action all over the world. It was developed as a 'battle taxi', conveying infantry to the combat zone and protecting them en route rather than providing direct support in the manner of a modern infantry combat vehicle. However, the M113 was instrumental in the development of such vehicles. Today's heavily armed IFVs have their origins in field expedients to protect the exposed commander as he operated the vehicle's machine gun.

Lightly armoured

The M113 is essentially a lightly armoured box on tracks. Its slab sides are not efficient in deflecting enemy fire, and its aluminium armour is effective only against small arms and shell splinters. The vehicle is light enough to be air-dropped, but this feature is unlikely to be relevant in Ukraine. Even after replacing the M113 in front-line

M113

The M113 has proven highly useful in a great variety of roles, including acting as an armoured cavalry platform, such as this model here in Ukrainian service. Such a vehicle might be highly effective against infantry positions but is vulnerable even to outdated anti-armour weapons.

service, the US military retained it for all manner of specialist and protected logistics operations. M113s supplied to Ukraine may well slot into this role or may be locally converted.

Weapons carrier

The standard armament of an M113 is a 12.7mm (0.5in) machine gun operated by the vehicle commander. This can be augmented with additional machine guns to recreate the armoured cavalry assault vehicle (ACAV) configuration seen in Vietnam and later on peacekeeping operations in the Balkans. Mortar carriers or guided missile platforms are also a possibility.

M113

Weight: 12.5 tonnes (12.3 tons)
Length (with gun): 5.3m (17ft 5in)
Width: 2.69m (8ft 10in)
Height: 2.52m (8ft 4in)
Engine: Detroit 6V-53T diesel, 205kW (275hp)
Maximum Road Speed: 67km/h (42mph)
Armour Type: Min–Max Aluminium Alloy RHA 13–44mm (0.5-1.7in)
Crew: 2 (+ 11 troops)
Main Armament: 12.7mm (0.5in) M2HB Browning heavy machine gun
Main Gun Ammunition Stowed: 1300

Bradley IFV

Originally conceived as a replacement for the M113 APC, the Bradley evolved into a highly capable multirole platform.

The M2 Bradley is an infantry fighting vehicle (IFV) with a crew of three. It can carry eight personnel in the rear compartment and permits them to fire from behind armour using weapons developed from the M-16 rifle. These are of questionable value, however, since they are aimed through a vision block using tracer rounds but can burn through an entire magazine before the weapon is brought on target. Most M2 Bradleys have all but their rear firing ports sealed up.

The provision of short-range defensive weapons was intended to prevent swarming by infantry, especially in close urban terrain where the vehicle's primary weapons may not be useful. These are a 25mm (0.98in) Bushmaster cannon and tube-launched, optically tracked, wire-guided (TOW) anti-tank missiles, making the Bradley capable of destroying light armoured vehicles and engaging tanks successfully given the right conditions.

Bradleys in Ukrainian hands have reportedly done so.

Ukrainian Bradleys

The USA initially supplied 50 M2 Bradley IFVs to Ukraine and sent more later. In combat, they demonstrated their survivability compared to the older generation of APCs (such as the M113). Bradleys have taken disabling hits without their crew or passengers being killed, and in most cases the vehicle was repairable. On the other hand, most disabled M113s were write-offs. This ability to return vehicles to the fight is a significant advantage over forces required to make increasing use of older APCs.

Bradley IFV

Bradleys have given good service in Ukrainian hands, proving resistant to damage and surviving more or less intact even when rendered inoperable. In the longer term the ability to return these vehicles to service may prove extremely important.

Bradley IFV
Weight: 36.7 tonnes (36.1 tons)
Length (with gun): 6.5m (21ft 4in)
Width: 3.28m (10ft 9in)
Height: 3.38m (11ft 1in)
Engine: Cummins VTA-903T diesel, 447kW (600hp)
Maximum Road Speed: 59km/h (37mph)
Crew: 3 (+ 7 troops)
Armour Type: Aluminium RHA + add-on spaced/composite + ERA + side-skirts
Main Armament: 25mm (0.98in) M242 Bushmaster chain gun autocannon
Main Gun Ammunition Stowed: 900

ARTILLERY WEAPONS

Artillery seldom achieves decisive results on its own, instead acting as a force multiplier for other unit types. Traditionally, this has meant bombarding fortifications and artillery positions or attempting to break up enemy troop concentrations, and artillery formations have carried out these roles in Ukraine throughout the conflict. However, modern artillery projectiles offer a range of new options.

Standard high explosive shells are capable of demolishing infantry positions and represent the most common cause of casualties, either from direct blast effect, splinters of shell casing or secondary debris thrown by the explosion. They are not particularly effective against vehicles unless a direct hit can be obtained, and even then, often the effects are not fatal. However, the effectiveness of standard munitions is greatly enhanced by advances in targeting and guidance.

No army ever starts a war with sufficient ammunition, and most of what was available to both sides was unguided high explosive. Computerized targeting increases the accuracy of such munitions, making Cold War-era shells more effective than when they were produced. In addition, guided munitions are now available. These typically make use of inertial navigation and/or the Global Positioning System and GLONASS satellite systems. Shells are still fired from one set of coordinates to another, but the likelihood of landing within a small distance of the intended aim point – known as circular error probability (or CEP) – is vastly smaller than with unguided weapons.

Ukrainian soldiers fire a D-30 howitzer at Russian positions near Klishchiivka, Donetsk Oblast, Ukraine, August 2023.

Towed artillery

The basic function of artillery has not changed; to deliver a projectile to the target area while remaining out of reach of retaliation. The cheapest way to do that is by using a weapon that can be towed by almost any vehicle.

However, towed artillery has the drawback that it takes time to set up and to be readied for its next move, potentially creating a vulnerability to counterstrikes.

Most of the towed artillery used by both sides dates from the Cold War or is derived from designs created at that time. It was standard practice in the Soviet era to create artillery calibres ending in a 2, making it immediately obvious that ammunition is intended for artillery weapons rather than tank guns, which end with a multiple of five. The use of Russian artillery calibres makes it difficult for Ukraine to source ammunition, as NATO countries use a different calibre set.

Basic towed artillery and mortars are relatively cheap but lack mobility, whereas vehicle-mounted systems can 'shoot and scoot' to avoid counterattack. Mobility, when combined with long range and great accuracy, makes possible the artillery raid as a tactic. Mobile artillery can advance under concealment as close to the enemy's territory as possible, deliver

an accurate salvo on some high-value target and then retire quickly to avoid a counterstroke.

D-30/2A18

Designated 2A18 in Russian service but known as D-30 elsewhere, this weapon is a simple manually loaded 122mm (4.8in) howitzer capable of delivering chemical weapon shells in addition to standard munitions. It can be towed by almost any military vehicle and is readied for action by spreading the trail and lowering the central jack. This raises the wheels clear of the ground. Newer weapons have a redesigned baseplate and a more effective muzzle baffle but are near-identical in performance.

2A65 Msta-B

The 2A65 is a 152mm (5.98in) weapon derived from the older D-20 gun-howitzer. Vast numbers of the D-20 were produced and sold worldwide, making a reappearance possible if losses require it. In the meantime, the 2A65 is the standard towed divisional

---

122mm howitzer D-30

Crew: 7

Calibre: 122mm (4.8in)

Elevation: - 7 degrees to + 70 degrees

Weight: 3150kg (6945lb)

Range: 15.3km (9.5 miles)

Muzzle velocity: 690m/sec (2264ft/sec)

122mm howitzer D-30

The Russian-made D30 howitzer has played a part in conflicts worldwide since the 1960s. It is unsophisticated but relatively easy to move into position compared to heavier artillery weapons.

Ukrainian servicemen fire a 2A65 Msta-B howitzer during military exercises near the village of Divychky in Kyiv region, Ukraine, October 2016.

artillery piece in Russian service and has not been exported. It uses a typical split trail carriage and can be towed by a military truck.

The barrel length is 47 calibres, giving a range of 24.7km (15.3 miles) with standard ammunition. Extended-range shells are available, which increase this to 28.5km (17.7 miles).

2A36 Giatsint-B

The 2A36 is a 152mm (5.98in) weapon with a longer barrel than the 2A65, at 49 calibres. Whereas the 2A65 uses the same ammunition as its predecessor, the 2A36 uses a different design which is not compatible with other 152mm (5.98in) weapons. This gives a range of 27km (16.8 miles) with

standard ammunition, with rocket-assisted projectiles having a greater range variously given as 22km (13.7 miles) or 40km (24.9 miles). A heavier weapon than the 2A65, the 2A36 has a four-wheel carriage incorporating a hydraulic rammer to assist in loading.

2B16 Nona-K

The 2B16 is an unusual weapon capable of functioning as a howitzer or a rifled mortar. It uses 120mm (4.72in) ammunition compatible with Western artillery systems and is breech-loaded. Barrel length is 24.2 calibres, giving a range of 12km (7.5 miles) with standard ammunition. Mortar bombs can also be delivered, as well as HEAT rounds, rocket-assisted projectiles

and a laser-guided shell with a range of 9km (5.6 miles). The crew of five are protected by a light gun shield, which is asymmetric to provide shelter for the sighting system. The shield is effective against splinters and small-arms fire only. The 2B16 is primarily used by Russian air-mobile forces and has not been exported.

2A29 MT-12 Rapira

The 2A29 is a developed version of the T-12 anti-tank gun, which entered service in the early Cold War period. Ukraine and Russia both inherited large stocks of these weapons upon the breakup of the Soviet Union. The use of towed anti-tank guns in Russian mechanized and armoured formations

has provoked some questions; one possible explanation is that they are an anchor preventing an embattled force from easily disengaging and thereby providing a steadying influence. Other commentators have suggested a simpler explanation – they are cheap.

The 2A29 uses a 100mm (3.94in) smoothbore gun capable of firing armour-piercing fin-stabilized discarding sabot rounds, with a maximum range of 3km (1.9 miles). HEAT ammunition, with a range of 6km (3.7 miles), is available to tackle lighter armoured vehicles. Guns are also provided with a small quantity of high-explosive fragmentation rounds for 'soft' targets, which can reach targets 8.2km (5.1 miles) away using indirect fire.

M101 howitzer
Crew: 7
Calibre: 105mm (4.1in)
Elevation: - 5 degrees to + 65 degrees
Weight: 2260kg (4980lb)
Range: 11.3km (7 miles)
Muzzle velocity: 472m/sec (1550ft/sec)

L118 Light Gun
Crew: 6
Calibre: 105mm (4.1in)
Elevation: - 5.5 degrees to + 70 degrees
Weight: 1860kg (4100lb)
Range: 15km (9.3 miles)
Muzzle velocity: 617m/sec (2024ft/sec)

Although its 100mm (3.94in) projectiles are not effective against the frontal armour of modern tanks, the 2A29 may have outlived its planned replacements. These were the 2A45 Sprut-A and 2A45 Sprut-B, both 125mm (4.92in) weapons. A conversion kit allows the 2A29 to launch laser-guided 9M117 Bastion anti-tank missiles, with a maximum range of about 4km (2.5 miles).

M101

The M101 is a 105mm (4.13in) howitzer dating from World War II, with its origins going back to guns captured from German forces during World War I. Originally designated M2, then M2A1, it became a standard weapon among NATO countries and was widely exported elsewhere. Despite its age, the M101 has won favour with Ukrainian forces. It is light and easy to transport, sufficiently accurate and highly reliable. Its range of 11.5km (7.15 miles) with standard ammunition and 15.1km (9.38 miles) with extended-range shells is a limitation. However, this can be overcome with good tactics and some ingenuity. South Korea manufactured this weapon under licence and may supply Ukraine with additional examples.

L118 Light Gun

The British L118 Light Gun was accepted for service in 1973 and later adopted for US service under the designation L119. It has also been successful on the export market. It can be towed by a light military vehicle such as a Land Rover or equivalent. Like many artillery systems, it can use conventional ammunition or base bleed shells. These reduce drag by injecting gas into the low-pressure area behind the shell in flight, extending range. Maximum range around 19km (11.8 miles) with base-bleed ammunition and 24km (14.9 miles) with rocket-assisted projectiles. An inertial/GPS targeting system was added during mid-life upgrades, greatly simplifying the task of aiming the weapon. L118/L119s were supplied to Ukraine by the US, UK and Australia, becoming increasingly important as shells for local 122mm (4.8in) calibre weapons became scarce.

FH-70

The FH-70 is a 155mm (6.1in) howitzer which began development in 1962. The intention was to create a common artillery weapon for NATO

FH-70 howitzer

The FH-70 uses standard 155mm (6.1in) ammunition. This calibre was standardised thorough NATO for its balance of range, warhead size and logistics burdens. It will likely replace Soviet-era 122mm and 152mm weaponry in the future Ukrainian arsenal.

nations and for it to be in service by 1970 – hence the designation FH (Field Howitzer)-70. The need for ammunition commonality between allies was readily apparent and is no less important today. The programme ran into difficulties, with the US pulling out and the European partners pursuing their own modified goals. It eventually entered service a decade after the intended date.

Most towed artillery systems need to be hitched to a vehicle in order to move even a short distance, and many are too heavy to be manhandled by the crew. The FH-70 solved this problem by incorporating an auxiliary power unit which allows the weapon to be repositioned without the use of a towing vehicle.

The first examples were delivered to Ukrainian forces in May 2022, finding favour with their new users. This has implications for future weapon selections; Ukraine is more enthusiastic about implementing 155mm (6.1in) shell production than expanding the manufacture of 122mm (4.8in) and 152mm (5.98in) munitions.

FH-70 howitzer

Crew: 8
Calibre: 155mm (6.1in)
Elevation: - 4.5 degrees to + 70 degrees
Weight: 9300kg (9.15 tons)
Range: 24.7km (15.3 miles)
Muzzle velocity: 827m/sec (2713ft/sec)

M777 howitzer

As the war in Ukraine bogged down into trench warfare, artillery weapons such as the M777 regained a World War I level of importance, allowing enemy positions to be attacked at a relatively low cost – shells are much cheaper than guided weapons.

M777

One reason for the withdrawal of the USA from the FH-70 programme was a disagreement over the acceptable weight of the weapon. US planners wanted a gun that could be easily transported by helicopter, which was particularly important for marines and rapid-deployment forces. The weapon selected was the M198 howitzer, which was replaced in 2005 by the M777.

These weapons were among the hundreds of artillery pieces received by Ukraine. They are reportedly very effective but vulnerable to Russian counterstrikes, especially when operating from static positions for an extended period. Lighter 105mm (4.13in) guns have demonstrated an ability to evade counterattacks and keep fighting, which may make them overall more useful than their more powerful 155mm (6.1in) cousins.

M777 howitzer

Crew: 5
Calibre: 155mm (6.1in)
Elevation: - 5 degrees to + 70 degrees
Weight: 4182kg (9200lb)
Range: 40km (25 miles)
Muzzle velocity: 827m/sec (2713ft/sec)

MORTARS

As the war in Ukraine became more static, mortars became ever more important. Their short range and high arc of fire enable munitions to be dropped into enemy positions in a manner often considered much more personal than bombardment with long-range artillery. The standard infantry-portable mortars used in Ukraine include the Soviet-designed 82mm M-37 and 120mm M1943 weapons. These date from the World War II era but remain effective in their intended role as support weapons for infantry that do not require vehicles to redeploy and can be used from a trench.

More advanced mortars are in use, including the innovative 2B25. This 82mm (3.22in) weapon is very light and has an unusually short barrel, but is primarily notable for its lack of signature. Little smoke or noise is generated, posing a problem for enemy troops trying to locate the source of incoming fire.

MO-120 RT

A Ukrainian soldier of the 93rd Brigade covers his ears while firing a French 120mm (4.72in) rifled towed mortar (MO-120 RT) at Russian positions in Bakhmut, February 2023.

Self-propelled artillery

Though often using the same or very similar weapons as the towed variety, self-propelled artillery has the advantage that it can set up quickly, shoot and then move to an alternate firing position to avoid retaliation.

With relatively short-range systems, there will always be a limited amount of suitable firing positions within range of any given target, increasing the risk to artillery weapons and their crews. An armoured vehicle provides at least some protection, though the best defence is for the enemy to be unable to locate the weapon or target it.

These defensive advantages are more likely to be important in the Russia-Ukraine conflict than the offensive ones afforded by enhanced mobility. The ability to deploy in or cross rugged terrain is useful, but the nature of the conflict means that being able to keep up with a fast-moving mechanized infantry or armoured force is largely irrelevant. Engagements tend to be primarily infantry affairs with slow, grinding offensives and bombardment of static positions more common than sweeping advancements.

In such an environment, especially where there is combat in urban environments, armoured artillery weapons can provide fire support in

a way that tanks cannot. The high elevation possible on an artillery weapon enables targets located high in buildings to be engaged, making self-propelled artillery an effective – if overkill – solution to a situation where enemy snipers are operating on the upper floors of a tall building.

2S1 Gvozdika

The 2S1 was developed in Ukraine during the Soviet era and remains in service with Ukrainian forces as well as Russian reserve units. It is built on the chassis of the MT-LB light armoured vehicle, also developed in Ukraine, which is protected against small-arms fire and shell fragments. It is powered by a 224kW (300hp) diesel engine and, like many armoured vehicles of its era, is amphibious. Preparing for a water crossing requires about 20 minutes. The artillery weapon is the same as the one used in the D-30 towed howitzer and is compatible with all Russian-type 122mm (4.8in) artillery ammunition.

2S1 Gvozdika

The Russian armed forces field a wide array of weapon systems and vehicles, but reduce maintenance difficulties and costs by using the same weapon in different roles. At its heart the 2S1 Gvosdika is a D-30 howitzer, albeit one with improved mobility and protection.

2S1 Gvozdika

Weight: 16 tonnes (15.7 tons)
Length (with gun): 7.26m (23ft 10in)
Width: 2.85m (9ft 4in)
Height: 2.73m (8ft 4in)
Engine: YaMZ-238 N diesel, 224kW (500hp)
Maximum Road Speed: 60km/h (37mph)
Crew: 4
Armour Type: RHA
Main Armament: 122mm (4.8in) 2A18 howitzer
Main Gun Ammunition Stowed: 40

2S3 Akatsiya

Entering Soviet service in 1971, the 2S3 mounts a 152mm (5.98in) howitzer based on that used in the D-20 towed artillery system. Like most self-propelled guns and AFVs, the weapon has a bore evacuator fitted behind its muzzle brake. This extracts most of the fumes from propellant from the weapon before the breech opens, preventing them from escaping into the crew compartment. Such systems are not needed on the towed version of the weapon.

Its range is around 18.5km (11.5 miles) with standard HE-fragmentation ammunition and 24.5km (15.2 miles) with rocket-assisted projectiles. A variety of other ammunition can be used including high explosive anti-tank (HEAT) rounds, artillery-delivered mines and the 2K25 Krasnopol laser-guided projectile.

These can be used against precision targets including enemy vehicles on the move. Large numbers of 2S3 self-propelled guns were produced and many are still in service, though they are being replaced by the 2S19 system.

2S3 Akatsiya

Weight: 28 tonnes (27.6 tons)
Length (with gun): 8.4m (27ft 7in)
Width: 3.25m (10ft 7in)
Height: 3.2m (10ft 5in)
Engine: V-59 diesel, 388kW (520hp)
Maximum Road Speed: 45km/h (37mph)
Crew: 4 (+2)
Armour Type: RHA
Main Armament: 152mm (5.98in) D-22 (2A33) L/27 medium howitzer
Main Gun Ammunition Stowed: 40

2S3 Akatsiya

Self-propelled artillery can keep up with tanks during a rapid offensive, but this capability has not proven useful in Ukraine. However, the ability to 'shoot and scoot' enables artillery to evade counter-battery fire.

2S19 Msta-S

Like other Russian military vehicles, the 2S19 makes use of existing components. Its use of a T-72 engine in a T-80 chassis did away with the need to create new systems, though it imposed restrictions on the development process.

2S19 Msta-S

The 2S19 Msta-S is a self-propelled version of the 2A65 Msta-B howitzer. Entering service just before the collapse of the Soviet Union, it is built on a T-80 chassis but uses a T-72 engine. It is fed from an automatic loader and can use a range of 152mm (5.98in) ammunition including high explosive, High-Explosive Anti-Tank (HEAT), smoke, and illumination rounds in addition to nuclear and chemical shells. The 2K25 Krasnopol laser-guided munition can also be launched. Range is around 24.5km (15.2 miles) with standard ammunition and 36km (22.4 miles) with extended-range rounds. Russian sources claim a maximum range of 80km (49.7 miles) from the latest 2S19M2 variant.

The 2S19 was developed to replace the 2S1 and 2S3 vehicles in Russian service. It is powered by a multi-fuel-capable diesel engine and armoured against small-arms fire. It is in service on both sides of the conflict, including some Russian guns captured by Ukraine. Russian service vehicles are normally deployed in batteries of six, with three batteries to a regiment.

2S5 Giatsint-S

In Russian nomenclature, the '-B' designation indicates a towed weapon, while '-S' designates a self-propelled version. The 2S5 uses the same 2A37

M109 PALADIN

The M109 Paladin entered US service in the 1960s. It has been upgraded since, but remains a Cold War weapon. Nevertheless, examples provided to Ukraine have proven effective in combat. The gun uses standard 155mm (6.1in) NATO ammunition, which is easier to source for Ukraine than Soviet-era munitions, and the chassis has many components in common with the M2 Bradley. This slightly simplifies the extremely complex logistics and maintenance situation facing Ukraine. The vehicle's aluminium armour provides protection against small arms fire but as with all such weapons the M109's primary defence is the ability to redeploy quickly.

gun as the 2A36-B, with near-identical ammunition performance. It can deliver nuclear munitions in addition to conventional payloads. Loading is performed semi-automatically under the control of a loader who is located outside the vehicle during firing operations, from a carousel holding 30 rounds. The chassis is adapted from the GM-123, originally developed for the 2K11 Krug anti-aircraft missile system.

2S19 Msta-S
Weight: 42 tonnes (41.3 tons)
Length (with gun): 7.15m (23ft 5in)
Width: 3.38m (11ft 1in)
Height: 2.99m (9ft 10in)
Engine: V-84A multi-fuel diesel, 617kW (840hp)
Maximum Road Speed: 60km/h (37mph)
Crew: 5
Armour Type: RHA
Main Armament: 152mm (5.98in) 2A64 howitzer
Main Gun Ammunition Stowed: 50

2S35 Koalitsiya-SV

As with many ambitious and innovative projects, the 2S35 became more modest during development. Its two-barrel design was

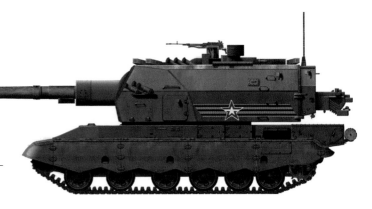

abandoned in favour of a more conventional weapon, which can be mounted on a variety of tracked and wheeled chassis.

2S35 Koalitsiya-SV

Weight: 46.7 tonnes (46 tons)
Length (with gun): 7.16m (23ft 5in)
Width: 3.4m (11ft 2in)
Height: 3m (9ft 8in)
Engine: V92 turbo-charged diesel, 750kW (1000hp)
Maximum Road Speed: 60km/h (37mph)
Crew: 3
Armour Type: RHA
Main Armament: 152mm (5.98in) 2A88 autoloading howitzer
Main Gun Ammunition Stowed: 60–70

2S35 Koalitsiya-SV

The 2S35 Koalitsiya ('Coalition') is so named because the original design had twin barrels. This feature was abandoned during development, but the name was retained. The artillery system consists of a 52-calibre 2A88 gun with 70 rounds carried aboard the vehicle. Range with conventional shells is 30km (18.6 miles) or 40km (24.9 miles) with rocket-assisted projectiles, and Russian sources claim a maximum range of 80km (49.7 miles) with specialist ammunition. The gun can also launch 9K25 Krasnopol laser-guided projectiles. Rate of fire is reported at 8 rounds per minute.

The chassis has much in common with the T-90 main battle tank and appears to house the entire crew within the main hull. This would require a high level of automation in the turret and is in keeping with other projects such as the T-14 Armata main battle tank. It is not yet clear how successful these endeavours have been. The 2S35 entered Russian service in 2020.

2S31 Vena and 2S34 Chosta/Hosta

The 2A80 is a breech-loading rifled gun/mortar that can deliver ammunition designed either for rifled

2S31 Vena

Weight: 8.7 tonnes (8.6 tons)
Length (with gun): 6.02m (19ft 8in)
Width: 2.63m (8ft 6in)
Height: 2.3m (7ft 5in)
Engine: 5D20 diesel, 179kW (240hp)
Maximum Road Speed: 60km/h (37mph)
Crew: 4
Armour Type: Welded aluminium
Main Armament: 120mm (4.7in) 2A51 gun-mortar
Main Gun Ammunition Stowed: 40

2S31 Vena

The 2S31 Vena can be landed by parachute and is amphibious, providing highly mobile artillery support in situations where conventional self-propelled guns would be unavailable.

2S34 Chosta/Hosta

The 2S34 was built on the chassis of the MR-LB light tracked vehicle, making it a highly mobile fire platform.

or smoothbore barrels. Range for standard ammunition varies from 5–9km (3.1–5.6 miles), and some extended-range projectiles can reach 17km (10.6 miles). The 3VOF112 Kitolov-2 laser-guided shell can also be launched.

This weapon is used on two vehicles, each intended as a higher-capability version of the 2S9 Nona. Both can engage targets using indirect fire or provide direct fire support at close range and feature advanced electronics. The 2S34 Chosta (or Hosta), built on the chassis of the MR-LB light-tracked vehicle, is similar to the 2S1 self-propelled artillery system while the 2S31 Vena is built on a BMP-3 chassis. Both are in service with the Russian army.

2S4 Tyulpan

The 2S4 Tyulpan ('Tulip') is also based on the chassis of the 2K11 Krug missile system. It mounts a 240mm (9.45in) breech-loaded mortar fed from two drums capable of holding a total of 20 standard or 10 extended-range shells. Range is 9.6km (5.97 miles) with standard ammunition and 19km (11.8 miles) using rocket-assisted projectiles. While relatively short-ranged and inaccurate, a 240mm (9.45in) mortar delivers a large warhead capable of destroying most positions. Laser-guided projectiles are available if greater precision is required.

In addition to high-explosive rounds, the 2S4 can launch chemical and, in theory, nuclear munitions. As part of the post-Soviet mutual disarmament agreement with the USA, all nuclear shells for this weapon were destroyed. At the outbreak of conflict in Ukraine, Russia had a small number of 2S4 self-propelled mortars in service and almost 400 more in storage. Those sent to Ukraine suffered heavy losses, largely due to their short range and general clumsiness. Taking 25 minutes to set up for firing and capable of delivering

2S34 Chosta/Hosta
Weight: 16.5 tonnes (16.2 tons)
Length (with gun): 7.57m (24ft 8in)
Width: 2.85m (9ft 4in)
Height: 2.83m (9ft 3in)
Engine: YaMZ-238 N diesel, 224kW (300hp)
Maximum Road Speed: 60km/h (37mph)
Crew: 4
Armour Type: RHA
Main Armament: 122mm (4.8in) 2A80-1 rifled gun-mortar
Main Gun Ammunition Stowed: 40

only one round per minute, the 2S4 is powerful on the attack but too vulnerable for the modern battlefield.

2S7M Pion/Malka

The 2S7M Pion, or Malka, consists of a 2A44 203mm (7.99in) howitzer mounted on a tracked chassis. This weapon was developed from the B-4 howitzer which was in production from 1932 until the end of World War II. Production of the 2S7 made use of

2S4 Tyulpan

Although impressive on paper, the 240mm 2S4 Tyulpan proved too vulnerable for operations in Ukraine. Even using extended-range rocket-assisted projectiles it is outranged by most of the weapons that might conduct counterbattery fire against it.

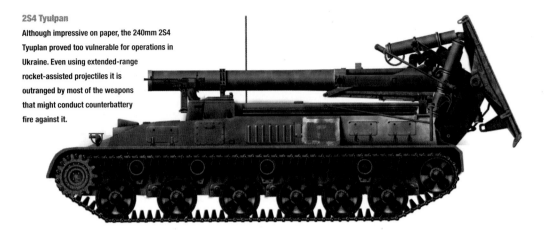

2S4 Tyulpan

Weight: 30.5 tonnes (30 tons)
Length (with gun): 8.5m (27ft 11in)
Width: 3.25m (10ft 8in)
Height: 3.2m (10ft 6in)
Engine: V-59 diesel, 388kW (520hp)
Maximum Road Speed: 45km/h (37mph)
Crew: 9
Armour Type: RHA
Main Armament: 240mm (9.5in) M240 gun-mortar
Main Gun Ammunition Stowed: 40

the wartime-era Barrikady production facility at Volgograd, with the result that its ammunition is not compatible with other 203mm (7.99in) weapons with a more modern origin. An upgraded version, designated 2S7M, is in use by both Russia and Ukraine.

In addition to HE and HE-fragmentation rounds, the 2A44 howitzer can fire cluster munitions and a concrete-piercing bunker buster shell. Nuclear munitions can also be launched. The original nuclear rounds were developed for the B-4 towed

howitzer, which was then in service, though improved versions were not compatible with it. It is possible a nuclear bunker buster round was put into development at some point but it does not seem to have been produced.

Panzerhaubitze (PzH) 2000

The German PzH 2000 has its origins in the multinational SP-70 programme, which like many other such endeavours ran into funding difficulties and eventually stalled. It has been widely exported, and a small quantity

2S7M Pion/Malka

Weight: 47.2 tonnes (46.5 tons)
Length (with gun): 10.5m (34ft 5in)
Width: 3.38m (11ft 1in)
Height: 3m (9ft 10in)
Engine: V-46-I turbo-charged diesel, 626kW (840hp)
Maximum Road Speed: 50km/h (31mph)
Crew: 7
Armour Type: RHA
Main Armament: 203mm (8in) 2A44 L/56 heavy howitzer
Main Gun Ammunition Stowed: 4

Panzerhaubitze (PzH) 2000
Advanced targeting systems enable
modern self-propelled artillery such as
the PzH 2000 to set up quickly for firing,
get their salvo off and leave the area,
reducing the window of opportunity for
counterbattery fire or other retaliation.

were delivered to Ukraine in 2022
with more to follow. The vehicle is
armed with a 52-calibre 155mm (6.1in)
howitzer, fed from an autoloader and
with a range of 30km (18.6 miles) using
standard ammunition. This increases
to 40km (25 miles) with base-bleed
ammunition and 56km (34.8 miles)
with specialist rounds, making PzH
2000 the longest-ranged tube artillery
system in the Ukrainian arsenal.

The survivability of the examples
sent to Ukraine appears to be good,
though there were reliability issues at
times. One factor in this was advanced
fire control, enabling guns to come into

action quickly, deliver their salvo and
move away.

An anti-armour projectile, SMArt
155, is available which delivers
submunitions to the target area.
These search for enemy armour using
radar and infrared sensors, delivering
an explosively formed penetrator
to the relatively weak top armour of
enemy tanks.

2S7M Pion/Malka

One of the heaviest self-propelled artillery
weapons in use, the 2S7M is designed to attack
distant targets of strategic importance, including
heavily fortified bunkers and command centres.

Panzerhaubitze (PzH) 2000
Weight: 55,000kg (121,275lb)
Length (with gun): 7.87m (25ft 10in)
Width: 3.37m (11ft)
Height: 3.4m (11ft 2in)
Engine: 745.7kW (1000hp) MTU 881 V12 diesel
Maximum Road Speed: 60km/h (37mph)
Crew: 5
Armour Type: RHA
Main Armament: 155mm (6.1in) L52 gun
Main Gun Ammunition Stowed: 40

Rocket artillery

Rocket weapons have advantages and disadvantages compared to tube artillery. The accuracy of individual shells is better than the accuracy of an equivalent rocket system.

While the first shell of a salvo, or the first shell from each gun in a battery, may arrive with little warning, the enemy will have time to seek cover before more arrive. This can be offset by using time-on-target attacks, with shells sent on differing trajectories timed to arrive all at once, but for the most part tube artillery is best suited to relatively precise sustained bombardment.

A large tube artillery attack requires considerable setting up whereas a rocket battery can dump a huge quantity of explosives into the target area very quickly after arriving at the firing point. Without the need for a lengthy setting-up period and preparation for moving afterwards, rocket systems can spend less time in predictable firing locations. Rockets are also relatively light and can be launched from simple rails on trucks and similar soft-skinned vehicles.

The fact that the world's major militaries use both rocket and tube artillery systems suggests that neither

is definitively better than the other and that both are desirable if the force is to maximize its capabilities.

Mobility

As with all weapon systems, artillery design is a trade-off between capability, mobility and cost. Artillery units do not normally face a direct threat from enemy ground forces but may be targeted by aircraft and drones. Counter-battery fire is one of the trickiest missions for artillery; one that has in the past required a level of artistry some militaries simply cannot aspire to. It has not been a characteristic of the Russia-Ukraine war. Mobility provides a good defence against most threats, but it comes at a price.

Apart from the obvious damage to the target, such tactics have a deeper effect on the course of the war. Until Ukraine obtained long-range artillery systems, such as HIMARS, Russian supply depots and command hubs were out of reach.

BM-21 Grad

Basic rocket artillery systems such as the BM-21 rely on volume of fire rather than accuracy. One of their key advantages is lack of warning – the whole salvo arrives in a very short period of time.

BM-21 Grad

Crew: 4
Calibre: 122mm (4.8in)
Rocket length: 3.226m (10ft 7in)
Rocket weight: 77.5kg (171lb)
System combat weight: 13,700kg (30,203lb)
Maximum Firing Range: 20.37km (12 miles)
Rate of fire: 2 rounds per second

Once attacks against them became a possibility, Russia was faced with a choice between expending thousands of soldier hours setting up protection for such installations, or accepting they might be destroyed by Ukrainian artillery. Whether by causing material damage or by tying up large numbers of soldiers on defensive works, long-range artillery weapons exerted an effect on the course of the war far beyond what their small numbers would suggest.

BM-21 Grad

The use of massed rocket artillery was a hallmark of the Soviet military during World War II, which was carried on into the Cold War with weapons such as the BM-21 Grad. Cheap and simple, consisting of a 40-rocket launcher mounted on a Uram 375D truck, the BM-21 has since been developed through numerous variants without really changing in function. Upgraded versions may be carried on a different truck and feature modern targeting systems allowing reasonable accuracy out to 40km (24.9 miles).

However, these are saturation rather than precision weapons, valuable for their intensity rather than accuracy. An upgraded version, designated Tornado-G, was deployed in Ukraine by Russian forces. Reportedly, some of these weapons were captured and turned against their former operators.

RM-70

Developed in Czechoslovakia, the RM-70 uses the same rockets as the former Soviet BM-21 but mounts them on a more modern 8x8 Tatra T-813 or T-815 truck. Both versions carry a

RM-70 multiple rocket launcher

The RM-70 rocket artillery system uses the same launcher and rockets as the BM-21, but makes them more effective with a high-mobility off-road truck chassis and immediate availability of reloads.

RM-70

Crew: 3
Main Armament: 122mm (4.8in) 40-barrelled rocket launcher
Rocket length: 5.2m (17ft)
Rocket weight: 307kg (666lb)
Range: 20km (12 miles)
Rate of fire: 40 rockets ripple fired in 20 seconds

A photograph taken in July 2022 shows a tail section of a 300mm (11.8in) rocket embedded in the ground. It was probably launched from a Russian BM-30 Smerch multiple rocket launcher during shelling of Kramatorsk, Ukraine.

BM-27/9K57 Uragan

The BM-27 rocket artillery system uses fewer projectiles, but of greater calibre. In addition to explosive and cluster munition payloads the BM-27 can be used to scatter mines.

BM-30/9K58 Smerch

Crew: 4
Calibre: 300mm (11.8in)
Rocket length: 7.6m (24ft 11in)
Rocket weight: 243kg (536lb)
Range: 70km (43.5 miles)
Rate of fire: 12 rounds in 38 seconds

complete reload for their 40 tubes, with automated loading. The original version has a lightly armoured cab, which the T-815-mounted RM-70/85 does not. These vehicles can be ready to fire within 2.5 minutes of arriving at the launch point and on the move 3 minutes after the last rocket is launched.

BM-30/9K58 Smerch

In service with both Ukraine and Russia, the BM-30 system was developed in the 1980s. It uses much larger rockets than the BM-21 system but fewer of them, compensating for volume of fire with greater individual destructive power and better targeting. Each launcher is accompanied in the

BM-27/9K57 Uragan

Crew: 6
Calibre: 220mm (8.66in)
Rocket length: 5.2m (17ft)
Rocket weight: 270 kg (600lb)
Range: 8–34km (5.0–21 miles)
Rate of fire: 12 rounds per minute

BM-30/9K58 Smerch

The BM-30 represents a new generation of rocket artillery capabilities. From high-intensity but rather random bombardment, newer rocket systems have become capable of delivering specialist munitions or, in this case, deploying a reconnaissance platform.

field by a reloader vehicle, with both carried on the same 8x8 military truck. Single rockets or salvoes of up to 12 can be launched. Standard payload is a unitary HE-fragmentation warhead but anti-armour submunitions can also be carried. Specialist rockets can reach ranges of 90km (55.9 miles), and an R-90 reconnaissance drone can also be launched. A modernized variant, designated 9A52-4 Tornado, is scheduled to replace the 9K58 in Russian service.

BM-27/9K57 Uragan

The 220mm (8.66in) BM-27 Uragan rocket artillery system entered Russian service in 1975 and has been widely exported. It has seen action with both sides in the Ukraine-Russian conflict. Single rockets or full salvoes can be launched out to a distance of 34km (21.1 miles) with standard munitions. Setting up to fire and getting ready to move off afterwards takes about three minutes. As with other Russian-designed rocket systems, the launcher vehicle is supported by one dedicated to reloading, designated 9T452.

Russia, Ukraine and other users have attempted to develop systems to replace the BM-27 but not all of them have made it to the deployment stage.

Uragan-1M

The Uragan-1M is a multi-calibre rocket system designed to replace older Russian rocket artillery. Mounted on an 8x8 chassis, the Uragan-1M carries two pods containing either a total of 12 300mm (11.81in) rockets or 30 220mm (8.66in) rockets. The launch vehicle is designated 9A53 and is accompanied by a reloading vehicle designated 9T249. The standard 300mm (11.81in) rocket has a range of 70km (43.5 miles), with an extended-range variant reaching 90km (55.9 miles). In addition to HE-fragmentation warheads, the Uragan-1M can deliver chemical weapons, mines, incendiary and cluster munitions as well as thermobaric weapons.

TOS-1A 220mm Solntsepek

Referred to as a 'heavy flamethrower', the TOS-1A is a launch vehicle for thermobaric rockets, which generate

TOS-1A

Crew: 3

Main Armament: 220mm (8.7in) 30-barrelled rocket launcher

Rocket length: 3.3m (10ft 10in)

Rocket weight: 217kg (478lb)

Range: 10km (6.4 miles)

Rate of fire: 30 rounds in 15 seconds

TOS-1A

Thermobaric weapons are highly effective but controversial, as it is impossible to avoid attacking civilians within the area of saturation. Collateral damage is all but inevitable with such an indiscriminate weapon.

A Russian Army TOS-1A multiple rocket launcher and thermobaric weapon is seen during the annual Army Games defense technology international exhibition, May 2021.

a tremendous blast wave. The ability to deliver multiple warheads in a very short time permits saturation of a target area out to the weapon's maximum range of about 6000m (19,685ft). The original TOS-1 had 30 launch tubes, with the upgraded TOS-1A carrying 24. Both vehicles are built on a T-80 tank chassis but are armoured only against small-arms fire.

M270 Multiple Launch Rocket System

A few examples of the M270 MLRS system were supplied to Ukraine, providing a long-range strike capability that had until then been lacking. Controversy surrounded such transfers, especially over weapons that could hit targets inside Russia. The system can carry two MGM-140 army tactical missile system missiles with a range of 300km (186 miles) but normally carries six rockets in each of its two pods.

These can be launched in under 30 seconds with a range of around 70km (43.5 miles). Pods are quickly reloadable from a support vehicle that accompanies the launcher.

M142 HIMARS

The High Mobility Artillery Rocket System (HIMARS) blurs the line between rocket artillery – which is traditionally unguided – and guided missiles. It provides the firepower of the M270 on a more mobile wheeled chassis, enabling a HIMARS-equipped force to launch artillery raids in unexpected areas and to withdraw again before a countermeasure can be formulated.

Rockets are GPS-guided, enabling a precision strike out to about 70km (43.5 miles). This combination of mobility, range and accuracy has enabled Ukrainian forces to strike at Russian supply dumps and command facilities previously out of reach, imposing additional strategic problems.

M270 MLRS

Crew: 3
Calibre: 227mm (8.94in)
Rocket length: 3.94m (12ft 11in)
Rocket weight: 207kg (677lb)
Range: 32km (19.9 miles)
Rate of fire: 6 rounds in 45 seconds

M270 MLRS

The acquisition of long-range artillery in the form of the M270 system was of vital strategic importance to Ukraine, though the provision of the Army Tactical Missile System was hotly debated due to fears of escalation if used to strike targets inside Russia.

M142 HIMARS

The HIMARS guided rocket system may be the single most important weapon of the conflict, allowing Ukraine to influence a wide area from within its defended territory.

M142 HIMARS

Crew: 3
Calibre: 227mm (8.94in)
Rocket length: 3.94m (12ft 11in)
Rocket weight: 360kg (675lb)
Range: 32km (20 miles)
Rate of fire: 6 rounds in 45 seconds

ANTI-AIRCRAFT SYSTEMS

In addition to attacking combat forces, air power allows a modern military to strike deep into enemy territory, disrupting logistics and eliminating command and control facilities. Air attacks may also be directed at civilian infrastructure in the hope of weakening the national will. Air threats take many forms and require different solutions. Drones, missiles and attack helicopters are typically countered with short-range systems whereas fast jets require longer-ranged and faster weapons.

Air defence is not just a matter of shooting down anything that comes over the horizon. While that capability may be desirable, it is not realistic to expect air defences to be sufficiently strong everywhere. Instead, air defence may disrupt attacks by making pilots concentrate on not being shot down rather than delivering their weapons, or force enemy air assets to avoid some areas due to excessive risk.

Against piloted aircraft, the risk of loss can be an effective deterrent or disruptive factor, but drones and missiles can be seen as expendable. However, it is one thing to lose significant numbers of unpiloted vehicles to achieve an aim and quite another to simply waste them. Effective air defence can therefore be achieved by creating sufficient risk (or the perception of risk) to enemy air assets.

Ukrainian soldiers from the 93rd Mechanized Brigade fire a 9K35 Strela-10 highly mobile, short-range surface-to-air missile system (NATO reporting name SA-13 'Gopher') after spotting a Russian surveillance drone between Kostyantynivka and Bakhmut, July 2023.

MANPADS

Man-portable air defence systems (MANPADS) must balance effectiveness with cost and weight. They are required in sufficient numbers to provide adequate coverage over time, enabling a ground force to deal with or at least disrupt more than one air attack, and are important to morale.

During World War II, it was Soviet doctrine that enemy aircraft be engaged with all available weapons, even handguns. This barrage of lead was only marginally effective even then, but it was found to be more beneficial to morale than passively seeking cover. In the modern era, seeing missiles go up from nearby infantry forces has the same effect even if the target is not downed, and it contributes to the perception of risk.

9K32M Strela-2 (SA-7)

Known by the NATO reporting name SA-7 Grail, the 9K32M was developed during the Cold War to give infantry a measure of defence against strike aircraft. It is shoulder-fired and uses infrared tracking. However, in the basic version, this is only effective in the rear arc of an aircraft, where its hot exhaust can be clearly distinguished. It is also vulnerable to flare decoys. The upgraded Strela-2 missile has better sensors, allowing an all-aspect engagement.

9K36 Strela-3 (SA-14)

The 9K36, known to NATO as the SA-14 Gremlin, was developed from the Strela-2 and has a larger engagement envelope. The supersonic missile has an improved seeker that is more resistant to decoys than the previous versions.

9K310 Igla-1 (SA-16)

Developed from the Strela series, the 9K310 Igla-1, or SA-16 Gimlet, has a more advanced missile with greater resistance to countermeasures and

a larger engagement envelope. It entered service in 1981. The missile will attempt a terminal manoeuvre intended to detonate on contact with the target's fuselage.

9K38 Igla (SA-18)

Entering service in 1983 and given the NATO reporting name SA-18 Grouse, the 9K38 incorporates further resilience to countermeasures and a higher velocity. Unburned propellant is detonated by a secondary charge to enhance the missile's effects.

9K338 Igla-S (SA-24)

Known to NATO as SA-24 Grinch, the 9K338 incorporates further improvements that increase its engagement envelope to 6km (3.7 miles). It will seek an impact detonation but has a proximity fuse which is triggered on a close pass within 1.5m (4.9ft) of a target. As with other members

9K310 Igla-1

A Ukrainian serviceman holding a 9K310 MANPAD observes civilians crossing a destroyed bridge during the evacuation of the city of Irpin, March 2022.

of its family, Igla-S vehicle and helicopter mounts are available for Igla-S.

9K333 Verba (SA-25)

The 9K333 is a further development of the Igla series. It has a three-channel seeker for greater resilience against countermeasures. Early MANPADS weapons were designed to home in on the strongest heat source they could detect and were easy to defeat using decoys. More advanced seekers require emissions in the right intensity range and can compare emissions at differing wavelengths. Officially adopted in 2015, 9K333 is unlikely to be available in large numbers.

IMPROVISED AIR DEFENCE VEHICLES

Both sides have fielded improvised anti-aircraft systems, created by mounting machine guns or automatic cannon on whatever chassis was available at the time. This Ukrainian vehicle is about as basic as an air defence system can be. On the Russian side, contraptions created by mating old naval air defence turrets to armoured chassis have been observed. All of these weapons rely on volume of fire for effect, creating an additional logistics burden.

A Ukrainian soldier tends a twin anti-aircraft cannon in an area far from the front-line as the Ukrainian army conduct operations targetting Russian trenches in Donetsk Oblast, August 2023.

Starsteak

The British-developed Starstreak is a semi-active laser-guided weapon, unusual among MANPADS. This makes it immune to the usual flare decoys, though guidance does rely on a skilled operator. Instead of a single projectile, Starstreak launches three tungsten submunitions that travel at Mach 3–4 and are intended to damage the target by impact as well as explosion. Their high velocity makes these projectiles effective against light armoured vehicles. In addition to its MANPADs configuration, Starstreak is available in a lightweight three-round launcher and can be mounted on vehicles or helicopters.

FIM-92 Stinger

Developed in the 1970s, the FIM-92 Stinger has seen action in conflicts worldwide as it has progressed through a series of upgrades and improvements. The missile is infrared-guided, with an IFF (identification, friend or foe) system on the launcher to minimize the chance of blue-on-

FIM-92 Stinger

The original 'Stinger' entered service in 1981 and has been repeatedly upgraded since.

blue launches. The basic FIM-92A had a range of 4km (2.5 miles), which has increased with improved versions. Targeting, proximity detonation and resistance to countermeasures have all been upgraded to the point where the E and F models are capable of attacking small targets such as drones.

FIM-92 Stinger

Length: 1.52m (60in)
Diameter: 70mm (2.75in)
Launch weight: 10.1kg (22.25lb)
Range: 5000m (3.1 miles)
Launch preparation time: 8 seconds
Warhead: Impact-fused HE-fragmentation

ZSU-23-4 'Shilka'

In service since the 1960s, the ZSU-23 produces an enormous volume of fire.
It can engage both airborne and ground targets.

ZSU-23-4 'Shilka'

The ZSU-23 'Shilka' is in service with both Russian
and Ukrainian forces (the latter illustrated here). A
greatly upgraded Ukrainian variant, equipped with
Strela missiles in addition to its guns, never reached
the production stage.

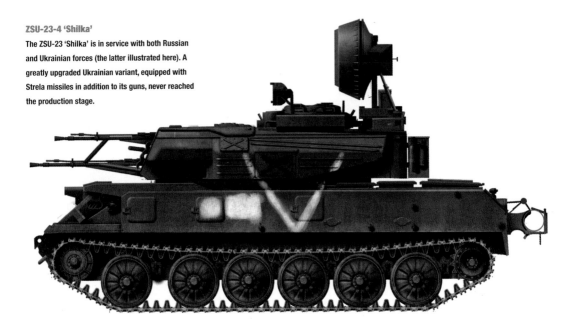

The ZSU-23 was developed to replace
the ZSU-57-2, the twin 57mm (2.24in)
cannon of which were not guided by
radar. The ZSU-23 traded potency
of individual shells for volume of
fire, with four 23mm (0.91in) cannon
delivering up to 1000rpm. Combined
with weapon stabilization and radar
guidance, this proved highly effective.

A series of upgrades and
modifications have taken place since
the introduction of this weapon
system. The Afghan version was
developed to engage ground targets
at high angles of elevation, and since
there was no air threat, the radar was
removed. Unlike its predecessor, the
ZSU-23 allows the crew to operate
entirely behind armour. Although
its protection is proof only against

small arms, this allows the ZSU-23
to function as a potent fire support
platform, which may be useful in the
cluttered terrain of Ukrainian cities.

ZSU-23-4M4

The latest version is designated
ZSU-23-4M4. In addition to its main
armament, it carries launchers for
man-portable air defence missiles and
has upgraded radar. Earlier models
of the ZSU-23 were rather slow
and lacked cross-country mobility.
The 4M4 version uses a hydrostatic
transmission, which transmits power
using hydraulic fluid rather than a
mechanical system, improving mobility.
The powerplant is a 209kW (280hp)
diesel, with an auxiliary power unit for
use when the engine is not running.

ZSU-23-4 'Shilka'

Weight: 19 tonnes (18.7 tons)
Length (with gun): 6.53m (21ft 5in)
Width: 3.13m (10ft 3in)
Height: 2.58 (8ft 5in)
Engine: V-6R, diesel, 209kW (280hp)
Maximum Road Speed: 50km/h (31mph)
Crew: 4
Armour Type: RHA
Main Armament: 4 x 23mm (0.9in) 2A7 autocannon
Main Gun Ammunition Stowed: 2000

2S6/9K22 Tunguska

Known to NATO as the SA-19 Grison, the 2S6 Tunguska combines gun and missile armament. It can engage airborne and ground targets.

The ageing ZSU-23 remains effective against low-flying aircraft and helicopters, but there is a limit to how far Cold War vehicles can be upgraded or modified. The Tunguska is constructed on a new chassis designated GM-352M, which is also used by the Buk and Tor air defence missile systems. It is powered by a 582kW (780hp) diesel engine located in the rear of the vehicle and is more mobile than its predecessor.

The original production model carried four missiles in pairs on the sides of the turret, but this was increased to eight on the 2S6M variant. In addition, it mounts two 2A38M 30mm (1.18in) cannon capable of delivering a maximum of 5000rpm. high explosive tracer (HE-T) and high explosive incendiary (HEI) ammunition can be mixed in belts feeding the guns.

The vehicle's surveillance radar can detect airborne targets out to a maximum of 18km (11.2 miles) and can track them within 16km (10 miles). The tracking radar has a maximum range of about 8km (5 miles).

The latest version, designated 2S6M1, has upgraded fire control and command systems and is more resistant to electronic warfare. It uses the 9K311M missile, which has improved tracking and a range of 10km (6.2 miles). These weapons are capable of engaging small, agile targets, including some models of cruise missiles.

2S6/9K22 Tunguska

Weight: 35 tonnes (34.4 tons)
Length: 7.9m (25ft 11in)
Width: 3.25m (10ft 8in)
Height: 3.35 (10ft)
Engine: V-46-4 diesel, 582kW (780hp)
Maximum Road Speed: 65km/h (40mph)
Crew: 4
Armour Type: RHA
Main Armament: 2 x 30mm (1.18in) 2A38M autocannon + 8 x 9M311M SAMs
Main Gun Ammunition Stowed: 1904

2S6/9K22 Tunguska

The Tunguska system was initially armed with 9K311 missiles, with a range of around 8km (5 miles). Equipped with 9M311M missiles, this is increased to 12–16km (7.5–10 miles). Guns can be fired on the move, but a missile launch requires halting the vehicle.

9K35 Strela-10

The 9K35 Strela missile system is intended to deal with short-range threats such as low-flying aircraft and helicopters. It can engage some types of drones and missiles.

Known to NATO as the SA-13 Gopher, the 9K35 is built on the MT-LB light armoured vehicle chassis. It carries four missiles in ready-to-fire condition, with eight more within the hull. It is powered by a 179kW (240hp) diesel engine and is amphibious without preparation. Rotation of the tracks propels the vehicle in water. The hull is armoured against small arms and shell splinters.

Drone destroyer

In the modern combat environment, drones and precision-guided missiles are as much a threat to ground forces as helicopters and aircraft, making short-range air defence even more of a priority. Although it was not built with such targets in mind, the 9K35 has received upgrades that – intentionally or otherwise – allow it and similar air defence systems to counter these new

9K35 Strela-10

The 9K35 Strela-10 can also launch 9K31 Strela-1 missiles. As the war continued, far longer than had been predicted, the ability to use older munitions stocks became increasingly important.

threats. This has required advances in target detection and tracking, and missile precision.

The 9M37 Arrow missile is capable of Mach 2 and has a range of 5km (3.1 miles). The latest version entered service in 1989 and is designated 9K35M3. It has been upgraded throughout its service life, increasing the engagement envelope and resistance to countermeasures. Effectiveness is further enhanced by an automatic target designation reception unit, which allows target information to be quickly relayed from the battery and regimental command posts.

9K35 Strela-10
Weight: 12.3 tonnes (12.1 tons)
Length: 6.6m (21ft 7in)
Width: 2.85m (9ft 4in)
Height: 2.3m (7ft 5in)
Engine: YaMZ 289 diesel, 179kW (240hp)
Maximum Road Speed: 62km/h (38mph)
Crew: 3
Armour Type: RHA
Main Armament: Four 9M37 surface-to-air missiles
Main Gun Ammunition Stowed: 12

Pantsir

Known to NATO as the SA-22 Greyhound, Pantsir is a shore-range gun/missile air defence system mounted on an 8x8 truck.

Emerging during the 1990s, the Pantsir system combines a twin 30mm (1.18in) cannon with 12 57E6 missiles. These include a booster stage, which is discarded two seconds into flight after providing extremely high acceleration, and a sustainer stage, which carries the 20kg (44.1lb) warhead to its target. The missiles are thought to have a hit probability of 75–90 per cent and can engage small and agile targets.

The engagement range for aircraft is 20km (12.4 miles), with subsonic cruise missiles engaged at 12km (7.5 miles) and smaller air-to-ground missiles at 7km (4.4 miles). The minimum engagement range with missiles is 1.5km (0.93 miles); at closer ranges, the Pantsir system relies on its cannon. The 57E6 missiles do not have their own seeker, relying instead on guidance signals from the launcher. The system can launch pairs of missiles at a given target or controlling four missiles, each with a different target.

Pantsir in Ukraine

The Pantsir missile system has been widely exported and has seen action in Ukraine. Fragments of a 57E6 missile were recovered from eastern Ukraine during the campaign against separatists, and footage later emerged of the system in use. Since the outbreak of hostilities, the Pantsir system has been deployed in Ukraine and to protect important buildings in Russia from drone attacks. New missiles are under development, including a smaller version designed to tackle small targets such as UAVs.

Pantsir

Air defence systems intended to accompany and protect tanks need similar cross-country performance, which requires a tracked chassis. For more general air defence tasks a wheeled chassis is cheaper and requires less maintenance.

Pantsir
Length: 3.16m (10ft 4in)
Diameter: 90mm (3.5in)
Launch weight: 94kg (207lb)
Range: 18km (11 miles)
Flight altitude: 15km (49,500ft)
Warhead: Multiple continuous rod; 20kg (44lb) containing 5kg (11lb) of explosive

---

Buk-M2

The Buk missile system is capable of engaging ground and maritime targets in addition to its primary role as an air defence platform.

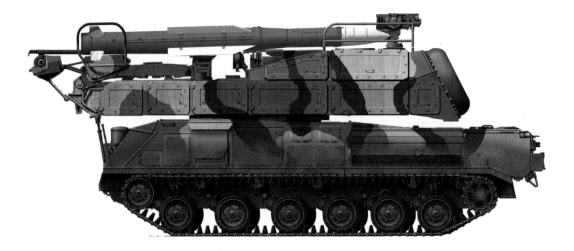

Development of the Buk system began in the 1990s, fulfilling a need to intercept tactical ballistic missiles and other airborne threats, including high-G manoeuvring targets. Early models were less effective against certain types of targets, such as hovering helicopters, but as the system matured, it became capable of engaging aircraft, helicopters, missiles and surface targets on land or at sea.

The launch unit and phased array radar system are normally mounted on a tracked chassis but can also be carried by a 6x6 wheeled vehicle. A towed version was at one point under development but has not entered service.

The 9M317 missile is guided by the launching vehicle, which can control four missiles at once. A standalone radar unit, which can be elevated on a 21m (69ft) telescoping pillar, assists in the engagement of low-flying targets.

Maximum range is around 45km (28 miles), though targets can be tracked beyond this distance. The 9M317 can engage targets which are manoeuvring at 12-G.

In service

The Buk missile system became notorious in 2014 when it shot down Malaysia Airlines Flight 17 over eastern Ukraine. It is operated by both sides in the Russia-Ukraine conflict and has successfully engaged fast jets. Ukraine struggled with missile shortages, a problem partially alleviated by adapting Sea Sparrow missiles – which also use semi-active radar guidance – for use with its launchers.

Buk-M2

High-capability air defence systems such as the Buk-M2 are priority targets. Since they are not designed to engage drones and other small aircraft they require protection by lighter air defence systems.

Buk-M2
Crew: 4
Length (missile): 5.5m (18ft 3in)
Diameter: 400mm (15.8in)
Range: 30km (19 miles)
Flight altitude: 14km (46,000ft)
Warhead: Radar proximity fuse; 70kg (150lb) warhead

9K330 Tor

Known under the NATO reporting name SA-15 Gauntlet, the Tor missile system provides short-range air defence against a variety of threats.

The Tor system is self-contained, with the launcher and radar system mounted on the same vehicle. This is a version of the GM-355 on the original system, while the improved Tor-M1 uses the GM5955 chassis. The launch vehicle is accompanied in the field by a transloader based on a 6x6 military truck. Reaction times are very short: typically 5–10 seconds from detection to launch. However, the vehicle must halt before firing, which can increase this figure.

Vertical launch

Missiles are vertically launched, using a cold-launch system which sends them 15–20m (49–66ft) clear of the vehicle before the missile's own propulsion ignites. Since the weapon

is not pointed at the target until after it leaves the launcher, its minimum engagement range is longer than that of more conventional systems. Depending on the variant in use, this distance can be as much as 2000m (6562ft). The missile can accelerate at up to 30gs, reaching Mach 2.8.

The Tor missile system is normally deployed in batteries of four vehicles, integrated with other weapon and sensor systems through a Ranzhir mobile command post. The M1 and M2 variants incorporate upgrades made since the system was developed. Among these is the ability to carry 16 9M338K missiles instead of eight 9M331s or 9M332s. Effective range with the 9M338 missile is 16km (10 miles).

9K330 Tor

Along with other modern air defence systems, Tor vehicles can be tied into a network commanded by a Ranzhir command vehicle. A mix of different systems can be used, optimizing defence against a range of long- and short-range threats.

9K330 Tor

Crew: 3
Weight: 34 tonnes (33 tons)
Length: 7.5m (25ft)
Width: 3.3m (10ft 10in)
Height: 5.1m (16ft 7in)
Engine: V-12 diesel 618kW (829hp)
Armament: Two 35mm (1.38in) autocannon

S-300/SD-300

The S-300 is a long-range air defence missile system in use with both Russia and Ukraine. The first version of the S-300 entered service in 1978 and was upgraded several times to create a large family of launchers and missiles.

The S-300V appeared in the 1980s, adding a ballistic missile interception capability. Guidance is by way of semi-active radar combined with an inertial navigation system in the missile itself.

The 9M83 missile has an engagement range of 75km (46.6 miles) for aircraft, while the 9M82 can engage at 100km (62 miles). Both use a 150kg (331lb) high explosive-fragmentation warhead.

Air defence in Ukraine

The S-300 and Buk missile systems were instrumental in shaping the air dimension of the conflict. They inflicted heavy losses on Russian aircraft early in the conflict, causing a move away from deep strikes using aircraft. The threat from long-range missile systems also forced Russian pilots to fly lower, increasing the effectiveness of lighter air defence systems. After the initial

S-300/SD-300

The S-300 missile system was developed to provide a countermeasure against tactical ballistic and cruise missiles alongside its more conventional air defence role. It is reported to be equivalent in performance to the US Patriot system, and able to intercept a target which is moving at up to 10,000 kilometres per hour (6200mph).

phase of the conflict, missiles and drones were used for long-range attacks, notably against the Ukrainian power grid.

The S-300 system proved effective against these attacks but suffered from a shortage of missiles. The solution may be to obtain NATO weapon systems of a similar capability such as Patriot. However, these are unlikely to be transferred in sufficiently large numbers to replace the 100 or so S-300 batteries with which Ukraine started the conflict.

S-300/SD-300

Length (missile): 7.5m (24ft 7in)
Diameter: 500mm (19.69in)
Launch weight: 1800kg (3968lb)
Range: 200km (124 miles)
Launch preparation time: 5 minutes
Warhead: 143kg (315lb) – will expel 19–36,000 metal fragments upon detonation

Flakpanzer Gepard

Built on the chassis of the Leopard 1, the German-made Flakpanzer Gepard has been transferred in significant numbers to the Ukrainian armed forces.

Development of the Gepard began in the 1960s, creating a relatively simple weapon system built around a pair of 35mm (1.38in) cannon with a range of about 4000m (13,123ft) using high explosive incendiary (HEI) ammunition. An armour-piercing round is also available, with a maximum range of 6500m (21,325ft). Gepard and similar weapon systems were intended to provide close-in defence against helicopters and low-flying aircraft, relying on volume of fire during a fleeting engagement with a fast-moving target.

Search and tracking

Like many similar systems, Gepard uses two radar systems. A pulse Doppler search radar is mounted on the rear of the turret, permitting a continual scan of nearby airspace. Contacts are interrogated by the IFF system and if not identified as friendly are transferred to the tracking radar mounted on the turret front. The search function is independent of tracking.

The Gepard was an export success, and although it is no longer in service with the German armed forces, it is still serving elsewhere. The examples transferred to Ukraine were obtained from various sources, including vehicles that had been awaiting dismantling after retirement. In Ukrainian hands, the Gepard proved highly effective despite its age, notably against drones such as the Iranian-made Shahed 136, which has been deployed in large numbers by Russian forces.

Flakpanzer Gepard

In Ukrainian hands, the Gepard is reported to have outperformed Russian-designed systems of a similar age and type. It is claimed that a Gepard's radar can track and target birds in flight.

Flakpanzer Gepard

Weight: 47,300kg (104,060lb)
Length: 7.68m (25ft 2in)
Width: 3.27m (10ft 9in)
Height: 3.01m (9ft 10in)
Engine: 623kW (830hp) 10-cylinder MTU MB 838 Ca M500 multi-fuel
Speed: 65km/h (40mph)
Road range: 550km (342 miles)
Crew: 4
Armament: Two 35mm (1.38in) autocannon

AIRCRAFT

The relative absence of Russian air forces in the early stages of the Ukraine-Russia conflict remains something of a mystery. Strikes were launched but on nothing like the scale expected. Possible explanations include complacency, worries about the strength of Ukrainian air defences and low serviceability rates resulting from corruption and lack of maintenance.

Whatever the reason, there was no overwhelming air attack preceding or supporting the ground invasion. Both sides lost aircraft, but – on paper at least – Russia was in a position to accept losses in return for a decisive victory. Instead, its air units made a rather poor showing and failed to exert much influence on the course of the war.

The air war over Ukraine took on a different character than expected. Ukrainian aircraft made their biggest contribution as launch platforms for cruise missiles such as the UK-supplied Storm Shadow, while drones and missiles carried out both small-scale attacks against local targets, such as groups of personnel or individual armoured vehicles, and bombardment of strategic targets.

Attacks on civilian infrastructure attracted international condemnation but had the effect of influencing the deployment of Ukrainian air defence systems. The necessity of protecting civilian infrastructure and populations from missile attacks translated to less air defence being available for the units engaged on the ground.

A Russian Su-34, with its distinctive 'stinger' between the exhausts. Although fast and manoeuvrable, the Su-34 has suffered significant losses over Ukraine.

Mikoyan MiG-29

Bearing a visual similarity to the Su-27 'Flanker', the MiG-29 is an air-superiority fighter that was gradually developed into a multirole platform.

First flying in 1979, the MiG-29 has progressed through a series of upgrades. The small fuel capacity of the original version, known to NATO as the Fulcrum-A, was increased on the C variant. Several export variants were created alongside the main family, eventually leading to the MiG-29SMT. Development was not without its problems, however. The installation of a large internal fuel tank in the spine of the aircraft created aerodynamic issues, so eventually a smaller 950L (209 gal) tank was installed.

Evolving armament

The original Fulcrum was designed to carry two medium-range air-to-air missiles and four short-range missiles, or 4000kg (8819lb) of other stores. These could include rocket pods, freefall bombs and submunitions dispensers, creating a basic air-to-ground capability. Nuclear munitions could also be delivered.

Improvements in electronics permitted later models of the MiG-29 to deliver precision-guided munitions, including laser-guided bombs and Kh-25 and Kh-31 missiles. Depending on the variant of the missile in use, this allows the MiG-29 to function in maritime strikes, precision ground strikes or suppression of enemy air defences (SEAD).

Ukraine war service

Both sides in the Russia-Ukraine conflict operate the MiG-29, and Ukraine has received additional aircraft from its European allies. Given that some of these allies have modified their MiGs to operate with NATO systems and that older airframes have been upgraded to match the specifications of newer models, the exact capabilities of any given example can vary.

Mikoyan MiG-29

'07 Blue' is one of over 200 MiG-29s still in the Russian inventory. The Russian Air Force version is typically armed with eight long-range air-to-air missiles; six R-73E short-range air-to-air missiles; four KAB-500Kr/KAB-500L guided bombs; and a 30mm Gsh-301 cannon.

Mikoyan MiG-29

Weight (maximum take-off): 19,700kg (43,431lb)

Dimensions: Length 16.28m (53ft 5in), Wingspan 11.41m (37ft 5in), Height 4.73m (15ft 6in)

Powerplant: Two Klimov/St Petersburg RD-33 (izdeliye 88) turbofans each rated at 49.42kN (11,100lbf) dry, and 81.4kN (18,300lbf) with after-burning

Maximum speed: 2400km/h (1491mph)

Range: 2100km (1305 miles) with under-fuselage drop tank

Ceiling: 18,000m (59,050ft)

Crew: 1

Armament: One 30mm (1.18in) Gryazev-Shipunov GSh-301 autocannon in the port leading-edge root extension; up to 4000kg (8800lb) of weapons and stores

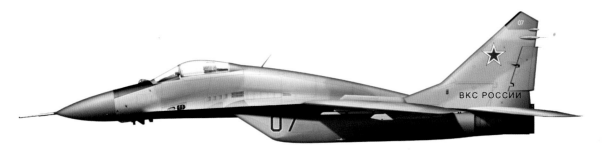

Sukhoi Su-24M

The Su-24 entered service in 1975, proceeding through a series of upgrades and new models, with the definitive Su-24M appearing in 1983.

Developed at a time when there was a real expectation of widespread tactical nuclear warfare, the Su-24 (named Fencer by NATO) was intended to deliver either nuclear or conventional munitions. Its variable-geometry wings permit a low take-off and landing speed, improving short-field performance and increasing warload capability, but can be swept back to reduce drag for higher speeds in flight. 'Swing-wing' designs of this type were popular for a time but have not been sufficiently successful to become standard. The Su-24M has a longer nose than preceding variants and has seven pylons for external stores in addition to its internal six-barrel 23mm (0.9in) cannon.

Total warload is 7500kg (16,535lb), including two infrared-guided air-to-air missiles. Experience with unguided bombs and rockets in Afghanistan and Chechnya led to an upgrade programme that reportedly made unguided munitions vastly more accurate.

Fencers in Ukraine

At the outbreak of the conflict in Ukraine, both sides possessed Su-24s. Russia reportedly had around 150 serving with its air force and 25–35 in a maritime reconnaissance or strike role. Some of these aircraft were destroyed on the ground in Crimea and others crashed for various reasons. Ukraine's handful of Su-24s also suffered losses in action and were reportedly used to launch Storm Shadow cruise missiles supplied by the UK.

Sukhoi Su-24M

Weight (maximum take-off): 39,700kg (87,523lb)
Dimensions: Length 24.53m (80ft 6in) with probe, Wingspan 10.37m (34ft) fully swept, Height 6.19m (20ft 3in)
Powerplant: Two Lyulka-Saturn AL-21F3 turbojets, each rated at 108.36kN (24,361lb) thrust with afterburning
Maximum speed: Mach 1.35
Range: 4270km (2653 miles), with one inflight refuelling
Ceiling: 11,500m (37,730ft)
Crew: 2
Armament: One 23mm (0.9in) six-barrel GSh-6-23M cannon, plus a maximum external load of 7500kg (16,535lb) carried on seven external pylons, including tactical nuclear and conventional bombs, precision-guided munitions, submunitions dispensers, rockets and gun pods

Sukhoi Su-24

The Su-24 was developed at a time when several nations were enchanted by the idea of variable-geometry wings. Most of its contemporaries, such as the US F-111, have been retired from service.

Sukhoi Su-25

The Su-25 (Frogfoot) is a robust and highly manoeuvrable aircraft optimized for close air support missions. Its multiple underwing pylons inspired the nickname 'comb'.

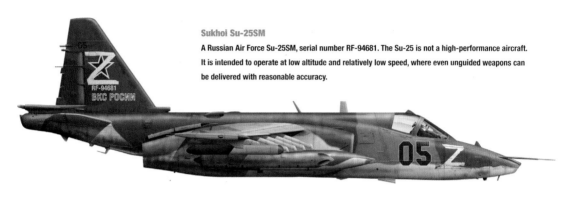

Sukhoi Su-25SM

A Russian Air Force Su-25SM, serial number RF-94681. The Su-25 is not a high-performance aircraft. It is intended to operate at low altitude and relatively low speed, where even unguided weapons can be delivered with reasonable accuracy.

Sukhoi Su-25

This Ukrainian Air Force Su-25 'Frogfoot' is part of the 299 Tactical Aviation Brigade, flying low-level missions over the Donbas region in eastern Ukraine.

First flying in 1975, the Su-25 was developed to meet a requirement for a highly survivable close support and strike platform. Both single-seat and two-seat versions were implemented, with the two-seaters capable of acting as trainers or switching immediately to a combat role.

Both versions have eight wing pylons capable of carrying an array of ordnance, plus a pair of small pylons for air-to-air missiles. A total of 4340kg (9568lb) can be carried, made up of freefall and guided bombs, rocket pods, gun packs and missiles. A twin-barrel 30mm (1.18in) cannon is also mounted. In addition, Russian Su-25s can deliver nuclear munitions.

Post-Soviet service

Russia and Ukraine, along with several other nations, inherited fleets of Su-25s after the breakup of the Soviet Union. It is no longer in production, though facilities to resume manufacturing remain in place. In 1999, Russia implemented a mid-life upgrade programme, producing the Su-25SM. The intention was to bring all Russian single-seat Su-25s up to this standard. Ukrainian aircraft saw

Sukhoi Su-25SM

Weight (maximum take-off): 19,000kg (41,888lb)

Dimensions: Length 15.53m (50ft 11.5in), Wingspan 14.36m (47ft 1in), Height 4.80m (15ft 9in)

Powerplant: Two non-afterburning Soyuz/Moscow R-95Sh turbojets each 40.21kN (9,039lb) of thrust

Maximum speed: Mach 0.82

Range: 1850km (1450 miles) ferry range

Ceiling: 7000m (22,966ft)

Crew: 1

Armament: One 30mm (1.18in) twin-barrel GSh-2-30 cannon, plus a maximum external load of 4340kg (9568lb) carried on eight main underwing hardpoints and two smaller pylons. Precision ordnance includes laser-guided Kh-25ML (AS-10 'Karen') and Kh-29L (AS-14 'Kedge') air-to-surface missiles and TV-guided KAB-500Kr bombs

Sukhoi Su-25UB

The Su-25UB is the twin-seater trainer version of the Su-25, used for training and evaluation flights of active-duty pilots. This Russian Air Force 'Red 79' has the serial number RF-91981.

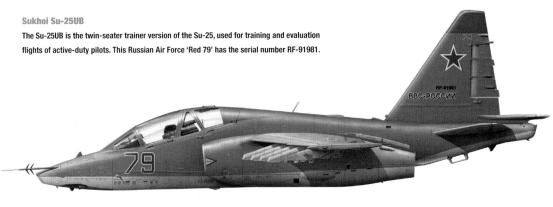

Sukhoi Su-25UBK

A Ukrainian Air Force Su-25UBK, the upgraded export model of the Su-25K. In addition to bombs and missiles, the Su-25's pylons can carry gun pods containing twin-barrel GSh-23 23mm guns with 260 rounds of ammunition.

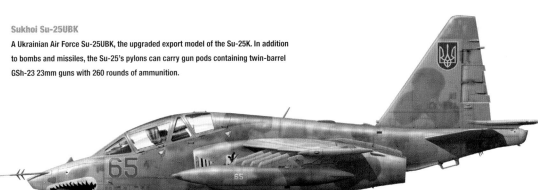

action against separatist forces in the east of the country in 2014–15, and there are reports of Su-25s in rebel hands during the conflict. Losses forced the withdrawal of Ukrainian Su-25s from the theatre, and both sides lost aircraft during the invasion of Ukraine by Russia.

Sukhoi Su-24UB

A Russian Air Force Su-25UB lands at Kubinka air base following the Victory Day parade, July 2020.

Sukhoi Su-27

The Su-27 (NATO reporting name: Flanker) began its career as an air superiority fighter with minimal ground-attack capability. It has since matured into a multirole platform.

The aircraft that became the Su-27 was conceived as a counter to the US F-15 Eagle, which also started as a purely air-to-air platform but developed into a potent strike aircraft. Its first flight was in 1977, with service beginning in 1984. Up to 1999, 645 single-seat Su-27s were built, with an additional 190 of the two-seat version. These were given the NATO reporting names Flanker-B and Flanker-C respectively.

Both Ukraine and Russia – along with other countries – inherited Su-27s after the fall of the Soviet Union. They carry an internal 30mm (1.18in) cannon plus up to 8000kg (17,640lb) of stores on 10 pylons. These can include infrared or radar-guided air-to-air

missiles, unguided rockets and freefall bombs. Russian Su-27s are also capable of delivering nuclear weapons.

Upgrades and sales

Russia launched an upgrade project in 2003, creating the Su-27M. Flankers of all versions have achieved considerable overseas sales, with China's J-11 fighter being developed from licence-built Su-27s. Ukraine was forced to sell off some of its aircraft due to maintenance costs and placed others in storage. Funds to return these to service became available at the outbreak of conflict with Russia.

Ukrainian Su-27s played a small part in the fighting against separatists before the Russian invasion due to

their limited ground-attack capability. Reportedly, Ukraine had 34 Su-27s available at the beginning of the conflict and has suffered several losses since then.

Sukhoi Su-27P

Weight (maximum take-off): 28,300kg (62,391lb)
Dimensions: Length 21.94m (72ft) without probe, Wingspan 14.7m (48ft 3in), Height 5.93m (19ft 6in)
Powerplant: Two Saturn AL-31F turbofans each rated at 122.58kN (27,558lb) thrust with afterburning
Maximum speed: Mach 2.35
Range: 3720km (2312 miles)
Ceiling: 18,500m (60,700ft)
Crew: 1
Armament: One GSh-301 30mm (1.18in) cannon, plus up to 4430kg (9766lb) of external stores on 10 weapons pylons

Sukhoi Su-27P

The Su-27 was developed as a heavy air-superiority fighter capable of escorting bombers. The Su-27P is the standard variant of the type (shown here in Russian markings), but without air-to-ground weapons control system.

Sukhoi Su-27S

The Su-27S was the initial production single-seater with an improved AL-31F engine. 'Blue 15' serves with the Ukrainian Air Force.

Sukhoi Su-30

Two versions of the Su-30 exist, with significant differences between them. Nevertheless, both are designated Su-30.

The Su-30 was developed from the two-seat trainer version of the Su-27, designated Su-27UB, but the two versions diverged quickly. Those produced in Komsomolsk-on-Amur are based on a variant created for export to China, while the more advanced version created in Irkutsk began as a project for export to India. This model is recognizable by its forward canards, which assist in manoeuvring.

Post-Soviet budget restrictions prevented more than a handful of Su-30s from entering Russian service early in the Su-30s career, though export success provided much-needed revenue for the Russian military sector. As a result, the aircraft delivered to the Russian Air Force and Navy in the past few years represent a design that has matured. The latest model is designated Su-30SM2, with older airframes upgraded to the same standard.

The Su-30 mounts a 30mm (1.18in) cannon in the starboard wing root and has 12 pylons for external stores. In its role as a heavy long-range fighter, it can carry radar or infrared-guided missiles, or up to 8000kg (17,637lb) of other munitions for ground attack. This includes the Kh-59 Ovod cruise missile, which has been used to attack targets in Ukraine. Despite the Su-30's ground-attack capabilities, it has primarily served in the air superiority role during the Ukraine conflict.

Sukhoi Su-30SM

This Russian Air Force Sukhoi Su-30SM 'Red 82' dates from January 2022. The Su-30SM is considered a 4+ generation fighter.

Sukhoi Su-30SM

Weight (maximum take-off): 34,000kg (74,957lb)
Dimensions: Length 21.94m (71ft 11in) without probe, Wingspan 14.7m (48ft 2in), Height 6.4m (20ft 11in)
Powerplant: Two Saturn AL-31FP thrust-vectoring turbofans each rated at 122.6kN (27,558lb) thrust with afterburning
Maximum speed: Mach 1.9
Range: 3000km (1864 miles)
Ceiling: 17,300m (56,758ft)
Crew: 2
Armament: One GSh-301 30mm (1.18in) cannon, plus up to 8000kg (17,637lb) of stores carried on 12 hardpoints

SUKHOI SU-34

Although clearly related to other members of the Su-27 family, the Su-34 (NATO reporting name: Fullback) has a much greater take-off weight. It is primarily deployed as a tactical bomber. Originally intended to create a strike version of the Su-27 with minimal modifications, the development of what became the Su-34 began in the 1970s. By 1994, when it received the Su-34 designation, the aircraft had gained a widened nose and enlarged tail 'stinger'. With a maximum load of 8000kg (17,637lb) of munitions on 12 pylons, the Su-34 has a wide range of guided and unguided weapons or pods containing sensors and electronic warfare equipment. Dedicated reconnaissance and electronic warfare versions were planned but never went into production. Instead, the Su-34 was deployed as what Russia calls a 'tactical bomber'. This role has no direct equivalent elsewhere; the distinction between heavy bombers and strike platforms is normally broad. In theory, the tactical bomber can conduct heavier strikes while retaining the agility and speed of a fighter. However, experience in Ukraine has shown that these relatively large aircraft are prone to losses from air defences. This is due in part to a shortage of precision-guided munitions.

Sukhoi Su-35S

The Su-35 is a development of the Su-27 family, incorporating advanced materials and improved electronics.

Sukhoi Su-35S

The Su-35 is a late fourth-generation (4 + +) air superiority fighter. It can undertake ground-attack missions but has been used in its primary role over Ukraine, where it outclasses all likely opponents.

During its development, the Su-35 underwent significant changes. Early models had forward canards, but these were deleted on the Su-35S. Thrust-vectoring engines and an advanced fly-by-wire system provided sufficiently good manoeuvrability that the canards were unnecessary. The result is an aircraft that visually resembles the original Su-27. However, it is internally different. Composite materials are extensively used in the structure of the aircraft along with an improved fire control system.

Multirole capability

Although conceived as a heavy fighter, the Su-35 is a multirole platform capable of carrying 8000kg (17,637lb) of stores in addition to its 30mm (1.18in) cannon. The pilot is equipped with a Sura-M helmet-mounted sight, which provides information and permits weapons to be aimed by looking at the

target. Manoeuvrable as the Su-35 is, it is quicker for the pilot to turn his head than the whole aircraft. In addition to allowing an over the shoulder missile launch, in air-to-air combat, the helmet sight allows a less predictable approach to ground targets.

The Su-35 saw action in Syria, mostly as an escort for strike aircraft. In the Ukraine-Russia conflict, it suffered losses but developed a reputation as a highly dangerous opponent that outclassed the older fighters available to the Ukrainian air force. Able to detect enemy aircraft

Sukhoi Su-35S

Weight (maximum take-off): 34,500kg (76,059lb)

Dimensions: Length 21.9m (71ft 10in), Wingspan 14.7m (48ft 2in), Height 5.9m (19ft 4in)

Powerplant: Two Saturn AL-41F-1S thrust-vectoring turbofans each rated at 137.3kN (30,865lb) thrust with afterburning

Maximum speed: Mach 2.25

Range: 3000km (1864 miles)

Ceiling: 18,000m (59,055ft)

Crew: 1

Armament: One GSh-301 30mm (1.18in) cannon, plus up to 8000kg (17,637lb) of stores carried on 12 hardpoints

and engage them at long range, the Su-35 is credited with multiple air-to-air kills.

Sukhoi Su-35

A Russian Air Force Sukhoi Su-35 (serial number RF-95242) takes part in a demonstration flight in Zhukovsky, near Moscow, during the MAKS-2015 airshow.

RUSSIAN BOMBERS

Russia has a large fleet of strategic bombers capable of reaching targets on other continents. These have played a relatively small part in the Ukraine conflict, serving as airborne launch platforms for cruise missiles. The Tu-160 'Blackjack', developed in the 1980s, is capable of supersonic speeds and can carry 20,000kg (44,000lb) of munitions internally with additional missiles on pylons. It is available only in small numbers, however. Ukraine inherited a handful from the Soviet Union but traded them to Russia or scrapped them long before the present conflict.

Visually similar to the Blackjack, the Tu-22 'Backfire' was developed in the 1970s. The original aircraft was disappointing, resulting in the improved Tu-22M (illustrated below). An upgrade programme in the 1990s came to nothing but the Backfire received improved electronic systems. Tu-22s have delivered missile strikes in Ukraine, and attacked the defenders of Mariupol with 'dumb' unguided bombs.

The Tu-95 'Bear' dates from the 1950s, and is powered by four turboprop engines. Though outdated and vulnerable to interception, the Tu-95 can launch its missiles from well outside Ukrainian airspace, enabling it to remain useful as a missile launch platform.

Russian bomber forces have been the victims of mysterious explosions, generally considered to be the result of drone strikes, while at their bases. Countermeasures include painted 'dummies' intended to distract attacks from the real aircraft.

Tupolev Tu-22M3 Backfire

Weight (maximum take-off): 124,000kg (273,373lb)

Dimensions: Length 42.46m (139ft 4in), Wingspan 23.3m (76ft 5in) fully swept or 34.28m (112ft 6in) fully spread, Height 11.05m (36ft 3in)

Powerplant: Two Kuznetsov NK-25 (izdeliye Ye) after-burning turbofans, each rated at 140.2kN (31,526lbf) dry and 245.18kN (55,115lbf) with after-burning Maximum speed: 2300km/h (1429mph)

Range: 6800km (4225 miles)

Ceiling: 14,000m (45,932ft)

Crew: 4

Armament: One 23mm (0.906in) Gryazev-Shipunov GSh-23 twin-barrel Gast autocannon in remotely controlled tail turret; up to 24,000kg (53,000lb) of bombs, missiles or mines

Tu-22M missile carrier

The Kh-22 is a large long-range anti-ship missile developed in the early 1960s which could be fitted with either a nuclear or conventional warhead.

Supply and logistical aircraft

While logistics is not the most glamorous aspect of conflict, it is vital to a military campaign. Air transport is relatively fast and can bypass most obstacles or enemy-created impediments, such as destroyed bridges, though there is always a risk of interception.

Attacks against the bridges between Russia and Crimea greatly impeded the movement of supplies on the ground, in turn hampering the efforts of Russian forces in the area. Ukrainian forces found it more difficult to prevent movement by air or sea.

Antonov An-26

Operated by both Ukraine and Russia, the Antonov An-26 is a simple and robust aircraft developed from the An-24 as a general purpose transport for personnel and cargo. The ability

to operate from very basic airstrips and to handle a harsh climate was a design requirement. The resulting aircraft was conventional for the type, with a high wing and twin turboprop engines.

Perhaps the most important feature of the An-26 is its powered rear door. The preceding An-24 was satisfactory in most ways but had a ventral loading hatch that prevented the airdropping of troops and supplies. Additionally, vehicles could not be loaded aboard. The An-26

Antonov An-26

Weight (maximum take-off): 24,000kg (52,911lb)

Dimensions: Length: 23.8m (78ft 1in), Wingspan: 29.3m (96ft 2in), Height: 8.58m (28ft 2in)

Powerplant: Two Progress AI-24VT Turboprop engines, 2,103 kW (2,820 hp) each

Cruise speed: 440km/h (270mph, 240kn)

Range: 2,500km (1,600 mi, 1,300 nmi)

Ceiling: 7,500m (24,600ft)

Crew: 5

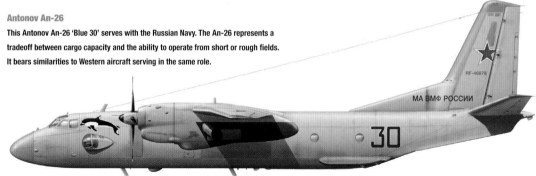

Antonov An-26

This Antonov An-26 'Blue 30' serves with the Russian Navy. The An-26 represents a tradeoff between cargo capacity and the ability to operate from short or rough fields. It bears similarities to Western aircraft serving in the same role.

Antonov An-26

Ukrainian Air Force Antonov An-26 'Yellow 05'. The powered rear door of the An-26 is one of its most important features. Loading and unloading are greatly facilitated, reducing turnaround time at forward airstrips, which may be vulnerable to attack.

Antonov An-30

Ukrainian Air Force Antonov An-30 'Blue 86'. The glazed nose of the An-30 is intended to facilitate its surveillance and aerial photography role. The aircraft are still capable of serving as cargo-haulers.

Antonov An-30

Weight (maximum take-off): 23,000kg (50,706lb)

Dimensions: Length: 24.26m (79ft 7in), Wingspan: 29.20m (95ft 10in), Height: 8.32m (27ft 4in)

Powerplant: Two Ivchenko AI-24TVT turboprop engines, 2090kW (2803shp) each equivalent

Cruise speed: 430km/h (270mph, 230 kn)

Range: 2,630km (1,630 mi, 1,420 nmi)

Ceiling: 8,300m (27,200ft)

Crew: 7

remedied this defect and was adopted by several militaries worldwide.

Antonov An-30

Also developed from the An-24, the An-30 was intended to serve as a reconnaissance platform in addition to its transport role. It gained a new forward fuselage and specialist features, such as a glazed nose, but retained its cargo handling equipment.

Relatively few were produced, but examples remain in Russian and Ukrainian service.

Ilyushin Il-76

The Ilyushin Il-76 entered development in 1966 and first flew in 1973. By 1978, the improved Il-76M had appeared, with a wider rear fuselage and additional fuel. More importantly, it had a greater load-carrying capacity. Later upgrades increased this further. Although it is a large-capacity, long-range aircraft, the Il-76 is capable of operating from unprepared runways with little support. Variants include a flying hospital and the Il-78 tanker. Given the relatively small operating area and the availability of Russian air bases close to Ukraine, tankers are unlikely to see much use in the conflict. The Il-76 can deliver 186 paratroopers or 305 infantry personnel. Its maximum takeoff weight of 210,000kg (462,971lb) includes a total of 60,000kg (132,277lb) of cargo on the Il-76MD-90 version, which has a new wing construction, improved engines and advanced avionics as well as self-defence countermeasures. It is armed with a twin 30mm (1.18in) cannon in the tail, though in recent years the trend has been to delete these weapons from large aircraft. Missiles are much more of a threat than close-range fighter attacks, which the guns might be able to counter.

Ilyushin Il-22M-11 Zebra

A Russian Air Force Ilyushin Il-22M-11 Zebra, November 2021. The Il-22M is a high-value airborne command post, of which only 12 were possessed by the Russian armed forces. Although kept out of range of Ukrainian weapons, one was shot down by Wagner Group mercenaries during their brief rebellion in June 2023.

Ilyushin Il-76MD

Weight (maximum take-off): 190,000kg (418,878lb)
Dimensions: Length 46.59m (152ft 10in), Wingspan 50.5m (165ft 8in), Height 14.76m (48ft 5in)
Powerplant: Four Aviadvigatel/Perm D-30KP series 2 (izdeliye 53) turbofans, each rated at 117.68kN (26,455lbf)

Maximum speed: 750–780km/h (466–485mph)
Range: 7800km (4847 miles)
Ceiling: 12,000m (39,370ft)
Crew: 5
Cargo: 60,000kg (132,277lb)

Ilyushin Il-76MD

A Ukrainian Air Force Ilyushin Il-76MD. Although the Il-76MD has more powerful engines and advanced electronic systems than its predecessor, its heavy lift capability is of limited use to the Ukrainian forces.

Ilyushin Il-78 Midas

In Russian hands, the Il-78 can deliver up to 56.9 tonnes (56 tons) of cargo to forces deployed in Crimea, bypassing the restricted road and rail access from Russian territory.

Kamov Ka-52

The Ka-52 Alligator, known to NATO by the reporting name Hokum, is a two-seat reconnaissance and attack helicopter.

Development of the Ka-52 began in the 1980s with the single-seat Ka-50 Black Shark, which is known under the NATO reporting name Hokum-A. Unusually for a helicopter, it is fitted with an ejector seat. The rotor blades are explosively detached when it is activated, their own momentum carrying them clear of the aircraft.

Helicopters are complex to fly as the main rotor produces torque that will spin the aircraft around its axis unless countered by a secondary rotor in the tail. The Ka-50 and its derivatives solve this problem by using a pair of contrarotating main rotors – the torque from one rotor cancels out that of the other. This gives improved agility over traditional helicopters.

Ka-52M

Development of the Ka-52 was slow and patchy until 2007, with the first aircraft delivered in 2011. In 2020, the improved Ka-52M first flew. This aircraft featured improved avionics and computers and is compatible with new precision-guided weapons. Nevertheless, unguided rockets remain a staple of the helicopter-carried arsenal and were reportedly used to attack Ukrainian shipping in 2018.

Short-range strikes

Despite losses, the Ka-52 has proven effective in Ukraine, notably when conducting short-range airborne counterattacks against advancing Ukrainian forces. Its warload can be tailored to the task at hand, including unguided rockets and gun pods for 'soft' targets and guided anti-tank missiles for attacks on enemy armoured forces. Man-portable air defence missiles can also be carried for anti-helicopter work.

Kamov Ka-52

Weight (maximum take-off): 11,300kg (24,912lb)
Dimensions: Fuselage length 13.87m (45ft 6in), Rotor diameter 14.5m (47ft 6in), Height 5.05m (16ft 6in)
Powerplant: Two Klimov/St Petersburg VK-2500 turboshafts, each rated at 1790kW (2400shp)
Maximum speed: 300km/h (186mph)
Range: 460km (286 miles)
Ceiling: 5500m (18,045ft)
Crew: 2
Armament: One 30mm (1.18in) Shipunov 2A42 auto-cannon semi-rigidly mounted on starboard fuselage side; up to 2000kg (4409lb) of weapons and stores

Kamov Ka-52

The Ka-52 is a two-seat version of the Ka-50 'Black Shark' attack helicopter, which it was developed to replace. Hokums are finished in overall dark grey or this somewhat arid camouflage scheme of sandy brown and olive drab over bright blue undersides.

Mil Mi-8MT

The Mi-8 is a ubiquitous transport helicopter produced in great numbers since the Cold War. It serves in a variety of roles.

Development began in the late 1950s, with first flight achieved in 1961. The design proceeded through upgraded variants, with the last of the first-generation models retiring from Russian service in 2009. Specialist versions were used for medical evacuation in Afghanistan, along with the Mi-8TV (Hip-C) armed variant. Experience in Afghanistan was incorporated into later models, notably the provision of a sliding door in the starboard side of the fuselage for rapid assault operations.

Armed and transport variants

The transport variant is designated Mi-8T (Hip-C), while the Mi-8TB (Hip-E) is armed for the gunship role. An upgraded version with a more powerful engine, designated Mi-17 (Hip-H) for the export market, with many examples going into Russian service under the Mi-8MT designation. It is armed with machine guns and has pylons for external stores, including bombs and rockets in addition to anti-tank and air-to-air missiles. Countermeasures pods are often also equipped.

In the airborne assault or personnel transport role, the Mi-8 can carry 24 troops in addition to its crew of three. Variants can be encountered in a communications and VIP transport role, serving as artillery observation or mobile command posts or undertaking general utility tasks. A maritime variant is also in use, carrying out similar tasks to ship-based helicopters but from shore bases.

Mil Mi-8MT

Weight (maximum take-off): 13,000kg (28,660lb)
Dimensions: Fuselage length 18.65m (61ft 2in), Rotor diameter 21.29m (69ft 10in), Height 5.54m (18ft 2in)
Powerplant: Two Klimov/St Petersburg TV3-117VM turboshaft engines, each rated at 1491kW (2000shp)
Maximum speed: 250km/h (155mph)
Range: 680–690km (423–429 miles**)**
Ceiling: 6000m (19,685ft)
Crew: 3
Armament: Up to 4000kg (8818lb) weapons and stores

Mil Mi-8MT

A flight of Russian Mil Mi-8MT helicopters train somewhere near St Petersburg, Russia.

Mil Mi-24 and Mil Mi-35

Often described as a flying tank, the Mi-24 Hind might better be thought of as an airborne equivalent to the infantry fighting vehicle (IFV).

When the development of the Mi-24 began in the late 1960s, it was expected to accompany and support rapidly advancing armoured forces, providing mobile fire support and delivering troops to key objectives as part of a large-scale offensive. While its troop capacity is much smaller than the Mi-8, the Mi-24 is better protected and possesses vastly greater firepower.

Weapons load

As with many combat helicopters, the Mi-24 carries an integral weapon. On most variants, this is an autocannon or multiple mounted heavy machine guns. The Mi-24's distinctive stub wings support pylons for up to 1500kg (3307lb) of weapons. These include unguided rockets and anti-tank guided missiles as well as versions of man-portable anti-air missiles capable of engaging slow airborne targets (such as other helicopters).

Mil Mi-35

Although it is showing its age, the Mi-24 is still highly regarded for its reliability and cost-effectiveness. An upgraded version, designated Mi-35, went into production in 2005. The improved helicopter has the same general configuration but more advanced avionics, navigation and targeting systems.

Countermeasures

A 23mm (0.9in) cannon is mounted in a turret under the nose of the aircraft, with additional weapons on the stub wing pylons. The Mi-35 carries an extensive countermeasures and defensive electronic warfare suite.

Mil Mi-28N

The Mil Mi-28 is optimized for the anti-tank mission, possessing improved manoeuvrability, performance and survivability over its Mi-24 predecessor, with night-fighting capability. It suffers from many of the reliability problems of the original design. Mi-28s carry their stores on four underwing pylons. The standard anti-tank configuration comprises eight anti-tank guides missiles carried in eight-tube clusters.

Other weapon options include rocket pods, incendiary tanks, sub-munition dispensers, mine-laying containers and gun pods. Currently, more than 100 Mi-28Ns are in service with the Russian Aerospace Services (illustrated below). In combat the Mi-28 has not proved invulnerable, with at least one lost to a British-made Starstreak missile in the early months of the war in Ukraine.

Mil Mi-28N

Dimensions: Fuselage length 16.88m (55ft 5in), Rotor diameter 17.2m (56ft 5in), Height (without radar) 3.82m (12ft 7in)

Powerplant: Two Klimov/St Petersburg VK-2500 turboshafts, each rated at 1641kW (2200shp)

Maximum speed: 280km/h (174mph)

Range: 200km (120 miles)

Ceiling: 5000m (16,400ft)

Crew: 2

Armament: One 30mm (1.18in) Shipunov 2A42 auto-cannon flexibly mounted under nose; up to 2350kg (5181lb) weapons and stores

Drones

Unmanned aerial vehicles (UAVs) have become a staple of modern warfare in recent years. They range from tiny reconnaissance vehicles to capable attack platforms.

While the ethics surrounding autonomous armed drones are still under debate, the use of remote-controlled weapon platforms seems a little different to deploying artillery or aircraft to attack a target from a safe distance.

Switchblade

The Switchblade drone is small enough to be carried by infantry and is launched using compressed air, after which its wings unfold in a manner that inspired its name. The drone carries sensors for short-range reconnaissance and a warhead capable of attacking personal and light vehicles. The drone is not autonomous; the operator is in the loop and can abort an attack until its terminal

Switchblade 600
Weight: 15kg (33lb) (Switchblade 600)
Dimensions: Length: 130cm (51in); Diameter: 150mm (6in)
Powerplant: Autonomous; manual
Range/Endurance: 40km (25 miles) or 40 min
Service ceiling: 150m (500ft)
Speed: 113km/h (70mph) (cruise)
Weapons: precision-guided lethal missile

Switchblade
Switchblade and similar weapons are sometimes called 'kamikaze drones' and are portrayed as autonomous killing machines. In fact the decision to attack or not is made by a human.

Bayraktar TB2
Weight: MTOW 650kg (1433lb)
Dimensions: Length: 8.5m (27ft 10in); Wingspan: 12m (39ft 4in)
Powerplant: 105hp petrol engine
Range/Endurance: 27 hours
Service ceiling: 5400–7600m (18–25,000ft)
Speed: 220–130km/h (70–120 knots)
Weapons: 4 laser-guided smart munitions

Bayraktar TB2
Drones such as Bayraktar offer the capability to get weapons to the launch point without risking a human pilot. Their small size makes them difficult to detect and counter.

phase. The original Switchblade was redesignated Switchblade 300 when the Switchblade 600, a larger anti-armour version, was introduced.

Bayraktar TB2

First flying in 2009, the TB2 is a medium-altitude combat drone manufactured in Turkey. It was used with success in the Syrian conflict, where it is reported to have destroyed Russian-made Pantsir air defence systems. In Ukrainian service, the drones were first used against separatist forces in 2020 and saw extensive use after the Russian invasion.

The drone has a maximum weapons load of 150kg (330.7lb) and uses the lightweight MAM family of missiles. The MAM missile family is laser-guided. The MAM-C has a range

of 8km (5 miles), MAM-L 15km (9.3 miles) and MAM-T 30–80km (18.6–49.7 miles). HE-Fragmentation, thermobaric and anti-armour warheads can be carried, depending on the mission.

Orlan-10

The Orlan-10 reconnaissance UAV was first deployed by Russian forces in Syria. It is launched from a catapult and lands with the assistance of a parachute. The modular payload can be tailored to the mission at hand, with reconnaissance, electronic warfare and data relay packages available.

Extensive use of these drones was beneficial to Russian artillery operations early in the conflict, and while losses were significant, the Orlan-10 is cheap enough to replace in large numbers. An upgraded version designated Orlan-30 carries a laser designator, enabling

---

Orlan-10

Weight: 9kg (20lb)
Dimensions: Length: 2m (6ft 6in); Wingspan: 3.1m (10ft 2in)
Powerplant: Petrol engine
Range/Endurance: 150km (93 miles)
Service ceiling: 5000m (16,404ft)
Speed: 150km/h (93mph)
Weapons: N/A

Orlan-10

Russian technicians work on an Orlan-10 reconnaissance UAV, December 2022. Reconnaissance drones such as Orlan have greatly increased the intelligence-gathering and reconnaissance capabilities of their operators, acting as force-multipliers for artillery and other conventional weapons systems.

Kronshtadt Orion

Larger drones such as Orion are more expensive but can operate at medium to high altitude where they may escape detection and where they are beyond the reach of most anti-aircraft weapon systems.

weapons to be guided without risking personnel or aircraft.

Lancet

The Lancet UAV is often described as a loitering munition as it is capable of spending an extended time searching for a suitable target. With a range of 50km (31.1 miles), it can be used for reconnaissance or strike missions and has successfully attacked high-value Ukrainian targets, such as artillery and air defence weapons. The Lancet is a small target with a low radar cross-section, making it hard to detect and engage with most of the available air defence weapons.

Massed small-arms fire can be effective, leading to some field improvisations such as multiple assault rifles fixed to a central pole to create a multi-barrel anti-drone gun.

Kronshtadt Orion

The Orion family of drones includes medium-altitude long-endurance (MALE) and high-altitude long-endurance (HALE) versions. The combat variant can carry up to four weapons with a total payload of 200kg (441lb) and has carried out successful strikes against Ukrainian vehicles. The reconnaissance and

Kronshtadt Orion

Weight (maximum): 1150kg (2,535lb)
Dimensions: Length: 8m (2 ft 3in);
Wingspan: 16m (52ft 6in)
Powerplant: 18650 lithium ion battery
Range/Endurance: 24 hours with 60kg payload
Service ceiling: 7500m (24,600ft)
Maximum Speed: 200km/h (120mph, 110kn)
Weapons: Vikhr-1V laser-guided anti-tank missile

surveillance version can operate at altitudes of 10,000–12,000m (32,800–39,370ft).

MARITIME DRONES

Ukraine has made successful use of uncrewed craft – maritime drones – to attack Russian warships. It is possible that small boats could be fitted with remote control systems to improvise such a weapon, but Ukraine has announced its intention to build an entire fleet of purpose-designed autonomous attack platforms. The drones reportedly have a range of 800km (497 miles) on a one-way trip and can function autonomously for up to 60 hours. Navigation uses GPS and inertial systems, with an optical system for target identification and attack.

Leleka-100

Weight: 5.5kg (12lb)
Dimensions: 1980mm (78in) x 1135mm (44.5in)
Powerplant: Electric
Range/Endurance: 2.5 hours
Service ceiling: 1500m (4900ft)
Speed: 70km/h (44mph)
Weapons: Ram-II loitering munition

Shahed-136/Geran-2

Known as Geran-2 in Russian service, the Iranian Shahed-136 drone uses a delta-wing configuration with a 'pusher' propeller at the rear. It is variously described as a loitering munition or suicide drone, with a 40kg (88lb) warhead that has been successfully used in attacks on Ukrainian forces.

Other members of the Shahed family include a variety of reconnaissance drones and Shahed-131, a smaller version of Shahed-136 known as Geran-1 in Russia.

Leleka-100

A Leleka reconnaissance UAV from the Ukrainian Defense Forces' 45th Brigade landing in the Donetsk region.

Eleron-3

Weight: MTOW 4.9kg (10.8lb)
Dimensions: Length: 0.6m (1ft 9in);
Wingspan: 1.47m (4ft 8in)
Powerplant: Electric motor
Range/Endurance: N/A
Service ceiling: 4000m (13,000ft)
Speed: 130km/h (81mph)
Weapons: N/A

Eleron-3

Russian soldiers launch an Eleron UAV on a military training exercise in 2015. The Eleron-3 has been deployed by Russian forces during the war in Ukraine to provide tactical reconnaissance.

APPENDIX: NAVAL WEAPONS SYSTEMS

Even though Ukraine and Russia share a long land border, the conflict has a significant maritime element. This is, on the face of it, rather one-sided, as Ukraine did not possess significant maritime forces at the outbreak of hostilities. At the collapse of the Soviet Union, ships of the former Soviet Black Sea Fleet were divided between Ukraine and Russia, with the latter receiving the majority.

The Russian Navy languished for many years with little new construction. However, Russia has a lot more vessels to work with and may be able to transfer ships into the Black Sea from its other fleets. Ukraine had only a handful of warships by 2022 and lost most of its maritime force in the early phases of the conflict. The handful of patrol craft remaining were insufficient to threaten Russian warships.

However, maritime warfare does not take place in isolation. In order to affect the situation ashore, Russian warships must operate within range of Ukrainian aircraft and missiles. The loss of a major warship is always a serious blow to the pride of a nation and the prestige of its leaders. As a result, the maritime conflict became something of a stand-off, with Russian forces controlling the Black Sea but unable to achieve decisive results without risking a sinking that could impact on morale and have serious political effects.

Ukraine has been offered warships by various donors, and the creation of a proper navy will no doubt be seen as necessary in the longer term.

Sea-launched Kalibr missiles can deliver a 450kg (992lbs) warhead within 3 metres (10ft) of a target from hundreds of kilometres away, enabling the Russian Navy to strike targets far inland.

Moskva

The flagship of the Russian Black Sea Fleet at the outbreak of hostilities was the Slava-class guided missile cruiser *Moskva*.

Laid down as *Slava* in 1976, this vessel was intended for blue-water operations against an enemy navy rather than land attack. In 1990, she began a long refit, from which she emerged in 1998 as *Moskva*. At the time of the invasion of Ukraine, *Moskva* was the flagship of the Black Sea Fleet.

Moskva supported amphibious operations along the coast in the early stages of the conflict, acting mainly as an air defence platform, as Ukraine possessed no vessels worth expending one of its 16 anti-ship missiles on. In addition to long-range air defence missiles and an array

of decoys and countermeasures, *Moskva* carried six AK-630 30mm (1.18in) close-in weapon systems. These represented the last layer of active defence against a missile threat, engaging 'leakers' that got past longer-ranged missile systems.

Despite the potency of her close-in weapons fit, *Moskva* was apparently struck by two Neptune anti-ship missiles fired from the shore. Russian sources have never confirmed exactly what happened, but *Moskva* caught fire and developed a serious list before sinking whilst under tow. Her loss was a serious blow to Russian prestige.

Moskva

Moskva was originally named *Slava*, and was the lead ship of its class. It has been suggested that damage control capabilities were poorly thought out in the design of *Moskva*, which may have contributed to its loss.

Russian and Ukrainian frigates

While less impressive than a guided missile cruiser, Russia's frigates are vastly more potent than anything Ukraine can currently put in the water.

With the sinking of *Moskva*, the role of flagship of the Black Sea Fleet fell to the *Admiral Makarov*, a frigate of the Admiral Grigorovich class. Developed as Project 11356, the Grogorovich class are new vessels constructed for the resurgent Russian Navy. Displacing 4064 tonnes (4000 tons), they mount a vertical launch system containing eight Kalibr cruise missiles backed up by a 100mm (3.94in) gun and extensive anti-air defences. The anti-submarine capabilities of these ships are irrelevant in a conflict with an enemy that does not operate submarines.

Land attack mission

The ability of its frigates to launch cruise missiles against land targets enabled the Russian Navy to strike deep inside Ukraine whilst remaining beyond the reach of a counterstrike. The key weapon in this mission, the Kalibr cruise missile, has multiple variants. Some can be launched from surface ships, some from submarines. There are anti-ship, anti-

submarine and land attack versions. The Kalibr missile reportedly has a range of 1500–2500km (932–1553 miles) and uses inertial guidance. Its standard warhead is 450kg (992lb) of high explosive, but it is possible the missile is nuclear capable. Kalibr is the standard Russian naval cruise missile and is carried by multiple platforms. It is installed on new-build warships and may be retrofitted to older vessels as part of a service life extension project.

Older frigates

Both Russia and Ukraine inherited Krivak-class frigates from the Soviet Navy. These were designed in the Cold War era as anti-submarine vessels and gradually developed into multirole platforms, with several variants appearing. One example was inherited by Ukraine and became the flagship of its small navy but was scuttled to prevent capture in 2022.

While the anti-submarine capabilities of the Krivak class are not relevant in the Russia-Ukraine

conflict, their 100mm (3.94in) guns and air defence armament enable them to carry out sea control operations and to support other vessels. It is notable that in recent years secondary armament on warships has increased, largely due to the move towards brown-water operations. The Krivak class carries multi-barrel 55mm (2.17in) grenade launchers for self-defence against small surface targets.

Small boat threat

The small boat threat has been taken seriously by world navies since the early 2000s and has gained a new dimension with the use of uncrewed surface vessels – 'drone boats' – packed with explosives. Whereas a ship operating in open waters has little to fear from small boats armed

Pytlivyy (Krivak II class frigate)
The Krivak class is a successful design that has progressed through several versions, some of which were intended for coast guard or KGB use. A variant, known as Talwar, was purchased by India.

with conventional weapons or making a suicide attack, venturing near a hostile shore is a different matter.

Naval guns and missiles are not effective against these threats; they are too low to the water and may be too fast to track with anti-ship weapons.

Fast-slewing autocannon and grenade launchers or manually operated heavy machine guns can engage them successfully.

The frigate *Sergey Kotov* reportedly defeated just such an attack made by Ukrainian maritime drones.

U175 Berdiansk (Project 58155)

The Gurza-M class is designated a 'small armoured artillery boat' in Ukrainian service. Armed with 30mm (1.18in) cannon, man-portable air defence missiles and a pair of anti-tank missiles, these craft are intended for a security role rather than taking on a blue-water navy.

Russian corvettes and patrol ships

In the post-Soviet world, the Russian Navy has developed a littoral combat capability that includes land attack using cruise missiles.

While the navies of the world have never relinquished their mission to dominate the open seas, littoral warfare has become increasingly important in recent years. Smaller and cheaper than a frigate, corvettes are not well suited to blue-water operations but may be superior to larger ships in restricted waters.

Karakurt class

The Project 22800, or Karakurt, class of corvettes represents current

Russian thinking in littoral combat. It carries eight Kalibr cruise missiles as well as a 76mm (2.99in) gun and two AK-630 30mm (1.18in) close-in weapon systems. Two diesel engines and a gas turbine combine to produce a top speed of 35 knots. The vessel can carry out patrol and security work or undertake anti-ship or land attack missions as required.

The primary means of air defence aboard the Karakurt class is the Pantsir air defence system, which combines

eight air defence missiles with a pair of 30mm (1.18in) cannon. In recent years, the Russian military has made efforts to create commonality within weapon systems, using the same missiles at sea and on land where possible and in this case deploying a whole weapon system in both arenas.

Buyan class

Designated Project 21631, the Buyan class is armed with a 100mm (3.94in) gun and Pantsir missile system in addition to vertical launch cells for Kalibr or Oniks cruise missiles. The latter were developed as anti-shipping weapons but have been used to attack land targets.

The missile has a range of 300km (186 miles), travelling initially in a ballistic arc before descending to a very low altitude for its final approach to the target. Although accuracy is not particularly good, the Oniks missile is difficult to defend against. It has also been used from K-300 (Bastion-P) coastal defence vehicles, engaging targets in Ukraine from Russian-held territory in Crimea.

Project 22160

Project 22160 is large for a corvette and is designed to undertake patrol work or protect naval bases and shipping in coastal waters. It is armed with a 76mm (2.99in) gun and mounted versions of the Igla man-portable air defence system (MANPADS). Quad launching tubes for Kalibr missiles are carried

under the flight deck, which retracts to allow the launching tubes to move to the vertical position.

Project 20380

Entering service in 2023, Project 20380 or Steregushchiy class uses composite materials in its superstructure to

reduce radar return, along with several new systems and techniques. The class is large, with a cruising range of 4000 nautical miles and a powerful armament. In addition to the usual 100mm (3.94in) gun, these vessels can carry eight KH-35 anti-ship missiles, which can also be launched from aircraft.

Soobrazitelny (Project 20380)
The Steregushchy class of corvettes is capable of undertaking anti-submarine warfare as well as surface action and air defence. Its configuration reduces radar cross-section whilst machinery is mounted on damped platforms to reduce acoustic signature.

RUSSIAN SUBMARINES

With no significant Ukrainian warships to hunt, Russian submarines of the Black Sea Fleet serve primarily as launch platforms for Kalibr cruise missiles. These can be launched from a torpedo tube to strike targets far inland. The ability to transit to the firing point underwater has some advantages, but overall the Russian submarine force has only a minor role to play in the conflict.

In September 2023, Ukrainian forces attacked the naval base at Sevastopol with Storm Shadow cruise missiles, heavily damaging an amphibious warfare vessel and a Kilo class diesel-electric submarine (illustrated below). Although the attack removed a missile launch platform, it may be that the weakening of Russian maritime logistics capability was more significant in the long run. The attack also underlined the threat to the Sevastopol naval base, making its continued use a difficult decision for Russian commanders.

UKRAINIAN MISSILES AND MARITIME WEAPONS

Ukraine inherited some warships from the former Soviet Black Sea Fleet, but by the beginning of the Russian invasion, these were mostly lost or otherwise out of service. Instead, Ukraine was forced to challenge Russian naval supremacy with missiles, maritime drones and small gunboats. The latter are insufficient to affect the course of the maritime campaign, but missiles and drones have achieved success.

Long-range missiles
Development of the Russian KH-35 missile began before the breakup of the Soviet Union, and afterwards, Ukraine continued to work on its own version. What emerged from this project was designated RK-360MC Neptun (Neptune), entering service just prior to the outbreak of conflict. Larger than the KH-35, and with a greater fuel load, these weapons famously crippled the missile cruiser *Moskva* and damaged the frigate *Admiral Essen*.

Tochka
The Tochka missile was developed in the Soviet Union as a replacement for the Free Rocket Over Ground (FROG) system of ballistic weapons. Known in the west as Scarab, the original Tochka rocket had a range of 70km (43.5 miles) and could deliver nuclear warheads. The upgraded Scarab-B version increased range to 120km (74.6 miles). Neither is very accurate, relying on inertial guidance only. Scarab-B has a CEP of 95m (312ft). This was sufficient to destroy a Russian amphibious warfare ship at anchor, but the Tochka missile could not hit a ship under way.

Storm Shadow
The Anglo-French Storm Shadow missile has a range of over 250km (155 miles), enabling Ukraine to strike at targets that were previously beyond its reach. It is pre-programmed, using GPS and terrain-following guidance to fly low and remain difficult to detect. Survivability is enhanced by a low-observable (stealth) construction. Since it is guided to a location rather than seeking a target, Storm Shadow is not capable of hitting moving targets but has demonstrated its effectiveness against fixed installations, such as command posts and supply dumps.

NSM
Poland supplied Ukraine with a quantity of NSM (Naval Strike Missiles) and launchers for them. These are operated by coastal defence units, which can redeploy as needed. Although the NSM has a relatively small warhead, its range of over 200km (124.3 miles) enables it to threaten vessels far out to sea. It uses GPS and inertial guidance to find the general target area and then activates an infrared seeker for the attack. This enables moving ships to be hit. Ukraine also received a quantity of Harpoon anti-ship missiles, but their status is unknown.

Storm Shadow

The Storm Shadow missile has its origins in a 1980s Franco-German collaboration. After Germany withdrew from the project the UK became involved, resulting in the British Storm Shadow and near-identical French SCALP EG missiles.

Storm Shadow
Length overall: 5100mm (16ft 8in)
Fuselage diameter: 1660mm (65.4in)
Wingspan: 2840mm (111.8in)
Warhead weight: 450kg (992lb)
Range: 250km (155 miles)
Speed: 1000km/h (621mph)
Powerplant: Turbomeca Microturbo TRI 60-30 turbojet
Guidance system: Inertial, GPS, TERPROM

Index

Picture Credits